SHADOWS OF THE PAST

SHADOWS OF THE PAST

A German SS Officer, his French daughter, and their story of hardship, heartbreak, resilience, and hope.

ANNITA RODGERS

Storytellers Publishing
Colorado, U.S.A.

Storytellers Publishing
An imprint of Journey Institute Press,
a division of 50 in 52 Journey, Inc.
journeyinstitutepress.org

Copyright © 2025 Annita Rodgers
All rights reserved.
(All photographs copyrighted to the author
except as noted for public domain images)

Journey Institute Press supports copyright. Copyright allows artistic creativity, encourages diverse voices, and promotes free speech. Thank you for purchasing an authorized edition of this work and for complying with copyright laws by not reproducing, scanning, or distributing any part of this work in any form without permission.

Library of Congress Control Number: Available upon request
Names: Rodgers, Annita
Title: Shadows of the Past
Description: Colorado: Storytellers Publishing, 2025

Identifiers: ISBN 978-1-964754-35-2 (hardcover)
ISBN 978-1-964754-36-9 (paperback)
ISBN 978-1-964754-37-6 (ebook/kindle)

Subjects: BISAC:
BIOGRAPHY & AUTOBIOGRAPHY / Women |
HISTORY / Wars & Conflicts / World War II / General |
FAMILY & RELATIONSHIPS / Military Families |

First Edition
Printed in the United States of America

1 2 5 13 22 38 39 47 61 95

This book was typeset in EB Garamond / Florania

Editing by Jessica Medberry, InkWhale Editorial LLC.
Cover design by WiggleB Studios

Dedicated to my loving husband Robert without whom this difficult work would not have been possible. His belief in me and his constant encouragement made me move on each day for several years to write.

Contents

FOREWORD	ix
PROLOGUE	11
PART I | HANS	**13**
WHERE DOES ONE BEGIN?	15
THE BEGINNING OF HELL	21
KILL OR BE KILLED	25
METZ, FRANCE	29
MARCELINE	36
THE KINDNESS OF A STRANGER	41
RUSSIA	46
THE LOSS OF HOPE	54
BERLIN	62
LITTLE ANNITA	67
BREATH OF FRESH AIR	71
1942	78
DO YOUR JOB	83
RETURNING TO FRANCE	89
LIBERATION BEGINS	94
NO WAY OUT	99
REPRIEVE	104
ESCAPE	111
CITIZEN OF METZ	116
WAR PRISONER	120
BETRAYAL	124
A FREE GERMAN IN FRANCE	133
DIVORCE	140
IRMA	147
MEETING ANNITA	152
NOVEMBER 1, 1965	157

PART II | ANNITA — 163

WHERE DO I BEGIN?	163
ANNITA CÉCILE WALBURGA	174
OMA & OPA	179
MEMORIES	184
CHRISTA	189
GEORGETTE	192
CÉCILE	197
THE HUNGRY YEARS	200
INHUMANITY	209
SIX YEARS	214
THE END OF THE NIGHTMARE	218
YOUNG LIONS	223
MY LIFE CHANGES AGAIN	227
AMERICA	234
MY FIRST DAYS ON THE FARM	238
ROBERT	248
CHALET	252

Foreword

Many books have been written, and movies and documentaries created about World War II. Their subjects are familar and often reflect the horrors of the war or the occasional heroic acts of an individual or small group.

What is less often the subject of these creations, are the stories of families caught in the crossfire, if you will, of this time period of global history.

This is one of those stories, but not the one you think it is.

This is a story about a family told from two disparate perspectives. One from the SS Officer who, as a young boy, is caught up in the Hitler Youth movement and joins the army, falls in love with a French woman, and starts a family during the war.

The other is from his oldest daughter who, for all intents and purposes, grows up without a father. She meets him for the 'first time' she can really remember when she is eighteen. Forty some years will pass by before she remembers the papers he gave her of his manuscript.

Thus begins her journey of learning, reflection, and understanding of this early part of her life. This is more than just a saga of a divided family and divided countries. This is a side of history we haven't heard before.

It is at once horrifying, heartbreaking, and touching. A tale of two worlds colliding that will leave you gasping and breathless while also giving you a glimpse into the day to day lives of those living through, and in, the war.

Told in two parts; the first through the perspective of the author's father, his German manuscript translated by her into English, which describes his journey into the army, his disolution with the war, and his ultimate desertion and capture as a prisoner of war where he begins writing his memoire from a jail cell.

The second, in the author's own words as a young girl trying to survive the horrors of the war as well as that of her single mother struggling to raise her family in the worst of all circumstances.

It is a poignant and stark look at the reality of life and simultaneously a story of redemption and hope amidst the chaos and aftermath of war.

At a time in the world where history is often being rewritten, *Shadows of the Past* is an rare glimpse into the true history from a unique perspective of someone who lived it.

I am sure you will find this dual-memoir to be one that will sit with you long after you read the final chapter.

Michael Jenet
Publisher
Journey Institute Press

Prologue

I am Annita Bosse, Hans's daughter.

When my father visited me in the US for the first time in 1972, he left his memoirs with me. I was in the process of moving to Colorado at the time and put the journal away, unread, in a box. I never remembered having it until forty-five years later.

It was first with curiosity that I started reading, then with deep emotions. Through my readings, I met a man I didn't know, the father I never had.

And now, so many years later, I have deep regrets that I never had the opportunity to let him know my feelings. Never having shared or talked about what both our lives had been, we had never really known each other and now never will.

Life had separated us from the very start in many ways. War, geographical distance, and most of all, grave misunderstandings. There is no turning back; I can only grieve a man so terribly misunderstood. So many questions will remain unanswered and the gaps never filled.

I don't want to know what he did or didn't do during those terrible war times, as nothing can be changed. I am grateful to have in my possession the words he wrote and left behind, and to have the chance to get to know him a little better.

He passed away tragically on April 29, 2001, in his eighty-first year. The will to live had left him long ago. He took his life, leaving only a brief note to his children.

I did my best to translate his memoirs. This is not a novel or a story. Nothing was modified from his original writings; his interpretations belong to him, and I have tried to keep the exact wordings and style in my translation from German to English. I respected every entry and wanted to keep the emotions and personal feelings as he wrote and expressed them.

Also, I kept the German names of cities and countries as mentioned in the original language, as well as military titles.

My only hope is to have done justice by bringing him back into the lives of his children and grandchildren.

FATHER, may you rest in peace. I miss you.

PART I
HANS

1
WHERE DOES ONE BEGIN?

It is the year 1945. I am a political prisoner of the French, at the Isle St. Sainsiforien, on the outskirts of Metz, Lorraine, France. Camp 141/1.

My name is Hans Willie Fritz Bosse.
Military status: Waffen-SS Sturmmann, Schutzstaffel (meaning an elite military unit of the Nazi Party that served as Hitler's bodyguard and as a special police force, and also a protection squadron). Sturmmann is a German name, translating as Stormtrooper. The Stormtrooper unit was first created in the year 1921.
Therefore, the abbreviation SS.

I was born in Frankfurt/Oder, Germany. October 3, 1920.
I am allowed paper and pencil once every other week. My writings are censored regularly. Writing keeps my sanity going in this dark cell and gives me the courage to go on. I have found a loose plank of wood under my bunk bed where I hide most of my writings, letting the guards have unimportant things such

as poems or letters to my family, which I know will never be delivered. I also know they hope to find out any political affiliations I might have had. Each time they walk in, I hold my breath and worry they'll find my hiding place. So far I've been lucky.

The war is lost for us Germans and I am luckier than most. Still alive and not in a hard labor camp, even though the work during the day is physically demanding and dangerous. Most of the other prisoners are assigned to clean minefields and rebuild roads.

I started these writings while in this prison camp and did not complete them until 1965; they have therefore been written over a period of twenty years.

I can write only at night by candlelight and have to be conservative with the candles. One candle a week is all we get. The nights are long and give me plenty of time to reflect on the past few years.

There is no grief at this point, nor sorrow or self-pity; those feelings have died in me long ago. What is left is a bottomless pit of emptiness. My dreams and the course of my life have been broken, my hopes and fears were slowly consumed from one end of Germany's Europe to the other. I am an empty man with only a huge amount of shame. To this day the taste of war is still like ashes in my mouth. What remains is the strong need to share my thoughts, experiences, tragedies and pain.

My only companions at this time are the rodents running along the walls, whose eyes seem to glow in the candlelight, and for some strange reason are rather comforting.

I hope whoever will read this someday, if my writings survive, will comprehend what it means to be young, foolish, full of hopes and dreams, and perhaps will understand where I came from.

It is difficult to find the right beginning and try to make some sense. Therefore, I will start where many young men my age came to know this world. Adventurous, happy, and carefree, with little knowledge of what the future held in store.

Times were beginning to change rapidly from what we knew. The days of being children, playing Cowboys and Indians, were soon to be behind us. Ahead lay the unknown, and I didn't have to wait very long to find out where destiny would lead me; it certainly was not what I had visualized. The politics and culture of my Fatherland had gone through enormous changes since World War I. Young people like myself were raised in a very strict and formal manner. Perhaps in other times and under different circumstances, life might have been different. To make it short, all of our dreams were taken from us with the clouds of a second world war looming on the horizon.

Figure1. Hans Willie Fritz Bosse

At the age of seventeen to eighteen, one could join Hitler's Youth Camps and the NSKK (Nationalistic Engineering Corps). I enlisted and was proud to be accepted. We attended meetings every Sunday and wore uniforms that made us look smart, powerful, and handsome in our eyes. Of course, we loved to be noticed by the girls who would turn around to look at us as we marched down the streets. I was seventeen then, good enough looking, I thought, and felt very important in that uniform.

On October 13, 1938, I joined the Waffen-SS Elite (Waffen meaning artillery). I had a choice to join or not to join; most of my friends did. I pleaded and begged my parents for days to let me join. Finally they gave in against their better judgment. Father, being in a high position at the Supreme Court, must have been influenced by his colleagues who had let their sons enroll. It was a prestigious position in the eyes of many.

We boys now belonged to Hitler.

Father refused to speak to me for a few days and Mother mumbled under her breath every time I was around her.

In time, things returned to normal.

I was sent to a training camp in Berlin on November 30, 1938, with the strong belief that I would help my country toward a better future. This is how one gloomy and rainy morning I found myself on board the train from Frankfurt/Oder to Berlin, leaving my hometown and parents behind for the first time in my life with mixed feelings and a very heavy heart.

Little did I know then that many years of sadness and loneliness were ahead from that day forward. I was still young and so naive.

I reported as a young recruit at 10:00 a.m. at my assigned military base camp in a pouring rain. I joined other young men waiting in line, and the first thing we went through was having our heads shaved. We were given a recruit uniform, a little large for my size. Boots, a revolver and a backpack.

Members of the Waffen-SS were required to have a tattoo on the left arm to verify their blood type, A, B, AB or O. The purpose of this tattoo was to be identified in case we were wounded, unconscious, missing our dog tags or in need of blood transfusion. It was a very small black-ink tattoo on the underside of the left arm near the armpit, no bigger than seven millimeters long. I guess as SS we were more valuable to the Reich than the regular army soldiers, who did not get tattooed.

In a few short days I learned that the golden dream I had imagined was of a different reality. We rapidly became men under difficult conditions. I did not like military life and had a hard time getting used to it in the beginning. Our dormitory consisted of bunk beds; the planks were covered with thin straw mattresses and no pillows. We were up most mornings at five o'clock or earlier. The days were spent running, jumping logs, and rolling in dirt and mud for training and exercises, among other things. In the evening I would fall into my bunk bed exhausted and did not mind the discomfort at all.

I remember some days waking at 3:00 a.m., walking twenty miles in the pouring rain carrying a heavy backpack, material and guns, and returning to the barracks eighteen or twenty hours later. Many times we were ordered to get out of our wet uniforms and, with just our shorts on, grab our toothbrushes and line up in the hallway. You may wonder what the toothbrushes were for? We had to clean the toilet bowls with them. This may sound laughable but it was by no means funny. Those same brushes would be used again later to brush our teeth. This is just a little episode, among others, of our training.

Thankfully, there was little time to brood over personal lives and petty things. It is not easy to explain what those first months were like in the Military Elite Force, Artillery Division. More than one of us, me included, lost the meaning of dreams, and our youth suddenly was gone forever. Some never made it. They were either expelled from the division or committed suicide.

What really hardened us the most was the cruelty of our training. At random, some of us were given a German Shepherd puppy to train. I never had a pet as a child and loved animals. I felt very lucky to have been given a dog. We could not help but get attached to those animals who, although fierce, were very loving and loyal to their masters. I named mine "Bubby" and he became my soulmate in many ways. He always knew my moods and was there to give me love and comfort when needed. He slept next to my bed and I could swear he understood everything I told him. Their training was very intensive and as hard as ours at times.

These dogs were incredibly strong and resilient. Bubby's eyes were always on me and I knew he would have given his life for me.

One morning, when Bubby was almost a year old, we were called out to the courtyard with our dogs. This was not unusual and many times was part of the training. We were ordered to line up, about twenty of us, with our dogs facing us. Then, to our horror, we were to pull out our pistols and shoot them point blank. Bubby sat there looking at me with his loving dark gray eyes.

So much love and trust in them. It was almost as if he knew what was about to happen. He put a paw on my boot as my eyes blurred with tears. I wanted to hug him, pet him and tell him not to be scared, tell him how much I loved him, but we were not allowed to touch them or talk to them.

I stood there, my hands shaking, unable to pull the trigger, until I received a blow between my shoulder blades that almost doubled me over. There was no choice, the gun went off. I saw nothing through my tears, heard nothing, and vomited.

The philosophy was that if we could kill a beloved animal, we would now be able to kill anyone or anything without qualms or hesitation. I felt so much hatred for the system at that time and wanted to run away as far as possible. How could we not become hard as ice in our hearts over time?

2
THE BEGINNING OF HELL

Time went by and the day came when I stood with my comrades, somewhat proud of the man I had become in a short time. We knew that our training had been for the good of the Fatherland, and we had been trained to take lives or lose our own lives.

Deep inside, I was not ready for the demands of this military life. However, I disciplined myself to not lose my identity, who I was, and where I came from.

We soon left the military training center. The few friendships we had built were sadly broken as we all were dispatched to different areas of Germany, destinations unknown. I was sent to Munich, Bavaria, where I

Figure2. Hans, cirqua 1940

appreciated a bit more freedom, if it can be called that. During the trip there, I realized what an error it had been to join Hitler's Youth Camps, and the pain I must have caused my parents.

In the days to come, we were allowed to leave the base compound for a couple of hours a week. I greatly appreciated those times to stroll the streets of the city to have a beer or two at a sidewalk café, or to watch people stroll by and dream of better days ahead. I was so sure that there would be no war and we would all get to go home. Munich was a beautiful city with pretty girls, beer flowing, and music everywhere.

However, that bit of freedom came abruptly to an end with the outbreak of scarlet fever on the base. Everyone was quarantined and we could, for the time being, no longer leave the confines of the camp.

As usual, I had to rebel. I was young with the desire for adventure in me and befriended a young man in my regiment. Neither one of us had contracted the disease, and we both decided that being locked up was too much to bear. We devised a plan to get out one night, if only for a few hours.

One evening after curfew we went to bed as usual, but kept our uniforms on. We pulled the sheets up to our ears, then waited for the lights to go out, and for the sergeant on duty to leave the dorm.

It was not an easy task to slide down from the second-story bathroom window. But we had planned it very carefully—two brains are better than one—and we made it without problems. It was a wonderful night out on the town. We met two pretty girls and promised them to return as soon as we could. We were back at the barracks before daybreak and roll call, drunk and happy.

Two weeks later, we decided to give it another try, knowing we could meet our girls at the dance hall. As we came around the side of the building, a voice called out and ordered us to stop. We kept on going as if we had not heard, and as we stepped outside the gates, the military police shot once in the air for warning. We ran as fast as we could and reached the city limits safe and sound, if a little out of breath. Certainly, we thought, they did not recognize us, and by morning there would be a change of guards. We made the most of the night out but were a little uneasy about what had happened. We soon found out what a sour apple we had bit into.

At five o'clock the next morning, we were still two kilometers from the base on foot and had no money for a taxi. We would miss roll call for sure and that meant trouble. We hailed a taxi anyway. Explained to the driver we were on orders to pick up an officer from the military base and bring him back to the train station, where he was to board a train to Berlin.

As the taxi neared the main gate of the base, we asked the driver to go to the side entrance of the barracks and let the meter run. We told him we would be right back with the officer. For good measure, I had him open the trunk for the officer's luggage. The side door was not guarded during the day and we made it back to our dorm without problems. But there stood trouble, the sergeant on duty with arms crossed and a dirty grin on his face. I will spare you the details, but we paid dearly for our escapades.

That month of April 1940 was the beginning of hell. My friend Fritz and I spent four days in the hole with only stale bread and water. We thought we would never survive, but we did. On the fifth day, we were brought before the military court, and our sentence was to be deployed to the eastern front lines in two months' time. Fritz and I were separated to different quarters.

I had no idea then that tragedy was soon to hit.

A week after the hearing, I found out Fritz had tried to desert but had been caught and brought back four days later. He was court-martialed and sentenced to death. In times of war, it was the sentence deserters received under the Führer's orders.

It was five o'clock on a dark, gloomy morning. The clouds hung low over the city of Munich. We were ordered to get ready and assemble in the courtyard to witness the execution of Fritz Manty. Terrible that day was, as we stood there to watch the Execution Commando line up.

Soldier Fritz Manty was brought into the courtyard to be shot to death for desertion. His eyes were blindfolded with a black cloth. He did not struggle, just let himself be led to the wall with his body hunched over. I stood stiff as a rod, my teeth biting into my lower lip, tears blurring my eyes. No one could've known how guilty I felt. Had it not been for me, he would not be standing there now. It was my stupid idea to go out at night that had led to this. I was only a few feet away from him and could see the white cross on the left side of his black and white striped prison uniform. The mark where the bullet would enter. What was going through his mind? What were his feelings? I thought I saw his lips tremble or mumble something.

There was a deadly silence as an officer's voice ordered, "PREPARE WEAPONS, ARMS IN POSITION, AIM, FIRE..."

One long, echoing sound resonated in the cold morning air. Fritz's knees buckled and his body hit the ground. An army doctor confirmed his death and we were allowed to go to the breakfast hall. Fritz was only eighteen years old, a child. I was sick to my stomach and my knees buckled. I would have collapsed without the help of another soldier holding me up.

That night I lay motionless on my army cot staring at the ceiling. No tears, no emotions, no feelings, I was drained. Something again had died in me. I knew I had crossed another border and nothing would ever be the same. The young Hans was gone.

3
KILL OR BE KILLED

Weeks passed with preparation for the front lines. It was early May when six other men and myself were to be shipped out. We did not speak to each other. We knew hell was waiting for us and perhaps Fritz had been the lucky one.

War had been declared on France in May 1940. I found myself with fighter troops in Northeast Germany in a little town called Westphalia, a very historic region of Germany. I felt like I was sinking deeper and deeper into despair, and there was no way out. Two days later, we left Westphalia en route to Holland.

It was there I experienced my first full-force baptism by fire around midnight, one mile over the Dutch border. Our regiment was attacked by aircraft. Before we could take cover, two of our trucks were blown up. Left and right, bombs were falling in horrible whistles and deafening explosions. Two of my comrades were killed in front of me; the war had just begun and had already ended for them. It was the first time I had seen soldiers fall in front of my eyes. I could not help but think that they probably had been lucky to die so quickly, to have been spared what horrors were to come. Rage was in my heart now, and I knew I was capable of anything to spare my own life. Kill or be killed.

It was all so new and frightening. Desperation washed over me in waves, but that also came to pass; as one learns very quickly, there is little time for inner feelings and fear when survival matters. Everything was happening so fast. There was no time to think. "Just keep moving," I told myself. "Just keep moving."

At the end of that first day of fighting, I saw my dirty face in a piece of mirror before collapsing on the bed. I did not recognize myself; it seemed I had aged ten years overnight.

No matter how exhausted I was, sleep would not come. Around and around in my mind danced images of death, of soldiers screaming, of wounded bodies and dead eyes staring at me.

After two hours of restlessness, we were called again to get ready. Ordered to pack, march on to Rotterdam and from there march to a small village outside Amsterdam. We arrived, cold, hungry, and tired. The fighting there was again a terrible sight, humanly impossible to grasp, impossible to describe what the horrors of war are all about. Bodies everywhere, wounded men's cries and moans, overturned trucks, fire, smoke, noise and chaos.

It took but six days to have Holland in the palm of our hands. We met with very little resistance and marched on to Belgium. There we joined with the rest of our troops, who had left ahead of us by a few days. However, there was no gift waiting for us in Belgium. We met face to face with French elite troops and it was worse than ever.

I had to admit to myself that the past few days, no matter how horrible they had been, were child's play compared to what we were now facing with the French troops as they were joined by British elite troops. It was a nightmare and a bloodbath all around as I crawled in the dirt and mud over bodies, some whole, some blown to pieces. If I had any idea what the meaning of war had been when I joined the army, I would have packed more underwear. Civilians were fleeing, bent under the weight of bundles. Babies were screaming in their mother's arms, chaos, chaos everywhere. At times the dust and smoke were so thick I had to put a kerchief over my mouth to be able to breathe. I was coughing uncontrollably.

Our advance was very slow, but we moved on and on. There was no time for feelings of any kind and I cannot go into the details of what I did and did not do. Survival was the master word. I was deaf from the sound of bullets ringing in my ears. My heart was thumping so hard in my chest that at times I thought it would rip it open. I just knew I would be shot at any time and felt there was no way any guardian angel could save me.

We reached our station late that evening. Again, the inferno we faced on the way is humanly indescribable. So many people lost their lives, innocent people, people who only believed in survival and saving their country. To this day, I still see the chaos, the blood, and hear the screams of the wounded. This is what I remember, and it will never, for as long as I live, be erased from my memory.

It was on a Thursday morning when I received orders to go by motorcycle as a dispatch rider to deliver a message to the advance troops. To reach them, I decided, foolishly, to take a shortcut through a meadow. I didn't get very far before fighter planes flew over and opened fire. I felt a sharp pain in my right upper arm and flew off the motorcycle. When I regained my senses, I saw the cycle was beyond use and blood was soaking my uniform sleeve. I took off my jacket, put pressure on the wound with my fist, and felt a big gap in the bicep area. This was the last thing I remember until I woke up in a military camp hospital.

On the evening of this grisliest day, I did thank my guardian angel for protecting me once more. I had not been killed, only hit by shell splinters in my upper right arm. I recuperated quickly and was sent back two days later to my command division.

Our troops were divided again. Sadly, I had to leave another comrade of mine, Wolfgang Bauer. We had become friends and shared a lot of thoughts and feelings. As we said goodbye and hugged, he said, "Don't worry, Hans, the wheel of fate has no bullet for us yet, we are lucky to be alive. Take care, maybe we will run into each other again in better times." He was right, we were alive.

4
METZ, FRANCE

I was to be stationed at a garrison in Metz, a beautiful city in the province of Lorraine, the northeast region of France. Metz was located an hour away from the German border and in the occupied German Military Zone, which, for the time being, was still safe for us. Though I was getting further and further away from my hometown and family.

It was raining cats and dogs when I arrived in Metz. Rainy days always have a way of making me sad and gloomy, and this was no exception. I had no idea what this city of Metz had in store for me and how it would forever shape my life.

The first thing I did when I arrived at my new barracks was inquire about my friend Wolfgang Bauer and find out where he had been sent. It took a couple of days to get the news. When the news arrived, it was a real blow; Wolfgang had been shot down the day after we parted. I was in shock, and one has to have experienced such emotions to understand. Again, a loss in my life; I felt drained of my own blood.

I could still hear his parting words so clearly. "Don't worry, Hans, the wheel of fate has no bullet for us yet, we are lucky to be alive. Take care, maybe we will run into each other again in better times." His words echoed in my brain as my throat filled with bile. Words I would never forget, words imprinted in my heart. Would there ever be better times? Would there ever be an end to it all?

Our new lodgings in the occupied zone were comfortable enough and centrally located.

Luck was on my side. A week after arrival, I received my first leave orders and could go home to Frankfurt/Oder for fourteen days. I almost jumped with joy. After so long, I would see my parents and hometown again.

I arrived home a couple of days later, and when my mother saw me for the first time in almost two years, tears of happiness streaked down her face. I will never forget the feeling of being held in my mother's arms again; I felt like a child. It gave me a feeling of safety, as if nothing could ever go wrong again.

My father, always a very strict man and in command of his feelings, had tears in his eyes.

I wondered at that moment what it must be like for so many mothers, wives and parents to have sons and husbands at the front lines, not knowing if they would ever see them again.

I am an only child, but was never spoiled by any means, in my opinion. My father, a respected magistrate in Frankfurt, was a stern man and an extremely strict and demanding husband and father. Because I was of a rebellious nature as a child, we often had rough times, butting heads with each other. Being disrespectful to a parent in those days was met with harsh punishment, such as a good whipping with a belt.

Somehow, I always found ways to get into trouble, such as once running away with a circus troop at the age of fourteen, only to be brought back home two days later by the police. My behind stayed sore for several days. I decided then to start my own circus and did some high rope walking between two buildings, charging my friends a fee to watch me. But my entertaining career came quickly to an end. I had to reimburse my hard-earned income and again had a sore rear end for a few days. Now, this seemed like nothing compared to what I had seen and experienced at the front lines.

Father also raised a few horses on a little property we had in the country, on the outskirts of Frankfurt/Oder. The Oder is a river, and Frankfurt is located on the east side of Berlin. Not to be confused with Frankfurt/Mein that most people are familiar with in the southern part of Germany.

I loved those times in the country when I was a boy, and being around horses. I learned to ride early in my childhood and was an accomplished rider by the time I was eight years old.

I always loved school. Poetry, writing and drawing were high on my priorities. My studies did not leave much time for such things, and I had to hide from my father to indulge in my hobbies. In his eyes, it was a waste of time. Being an only child, I felt lonely at times and would find refuge mostly in reading and writing.

Now this seemed all so far away. I had become someone else, someone I no longer recognized or liked. I had seen and experienced things many boys my age were spared to see.

The fourteen days at home were like heaven. Sleeping as long as I wanted, coffee in bed, Mother spoiling me from morning to night, wonderful meals, even Father letting his guard down and treating me like an equal. Time flew by and soon I was on the return journey to France.

I arrived back at my assigned barracks in Metz, France. I did not know how long I would be stationed there; things could change from one minute to the next. Meanwhile, I was a little safer there in an occupied French zone and further away from the front lines.

The following days gave me the opportunity to get settled, acquainted with new comrades, and familiar with the base.

Our daily duties were physically taxing, but we had most of our evenings free. I was not lonely; new friendships were in the making, but I missed my old friend Wolfgang, his sense of humor and bright smile. I still could not accept that he was no longer of this world.

I decided to spend my time off base to get to know the city of Metz. It was a very historic town with beautiful architecture, churches, remains of Roman ruins, parks, and quaint little neighborhoods. We were allowed to wear civilian clothes when off duty, which made it a little easier being around French civilians. I hoped I would not stick out and look too German and see hatred in people's eyes. We were occupying their country, after all, and we were the enemy.

I liked the provincial charm of the streets lined with cafés, the little shops, the flowers in the parks and, of course, the pretty French girls. I walked along the Moselle River lined with chestnut trees and visited the Cathedral of Saint Etienne, built in the 11th century, the Roman courtyards and the monasteries. It was a new culture to me; I loved hearing the French language, and I was excited to get acquainted with great foods and wines as well. The area of Lorraine and Alsace, being a German-occupied zone, gave me a sense of security and freedom. I walked for a couple of hours and decided to take in a movie, even though I could understand but a few words of French. Perhaps after, I would go for a leisurely dinner at a little restaurant.

I cannot recall what movie I saw, I only remember that for whatever reason, in the middle of the show, I suddenly broke into tears like a child. I was startled as I heard a voice at my side asking me if I was ill. Of course I was embarrassed and could not come up with an answer. Almost right away, I felt much lighter. A feeling I had not had in a very long time, and I almost wanted to laugh out loud. Perhaps it was a case of nerves and of constant controlled emotions.

I could not believe that someone cared enough to be concerned. I had not yet answered the person who sat at my right. I turned to see who it was in the darkness; I could only tell it was a woman with long hair. I answered that I was fine and thanked her.

When the movie ended and the lights came on, I saw it was a beautiful young girl. She got up without paying attention to me and walked toward the exit. I quickly followed her and was able to catch up and take a good look. Her long, blond curly hair caught the light of the sun; she was a little plump but with beautiful features. I tapped her arm lightly, and she turned and looked at me with such kind eyes that my knees turned weak. Again, I was speechless and just stood there.

We looked at each other and neither one of us spoke for a moment. I felt so awkward as I mumbled something about the movie in what little French I knew. I cannot remember what she answered as we started walking down the sidewalk, but it was in perfect German.

I found out that, although there was no flaw to her German, she was French. Her name was Eliane. She was from Paris, was an English and German translator, and was visiting her sister in Metz for a few days. Eliane looked older than I, perhaps by five years or so. I invited her to have a drink and was surprised when she accepted the invitation of a German.

We found a quiet little bistro and a couple of hours went by before I realized that I was getting close to my curfew. I certainly did not want a repeat of what had happened in Munich. I told her I had to go and asked if I could see her again, perhaps the next week? She accepted and wrote her name and address on a piece of paper. I tried to kiss her goodbye, but she gently pushed me away. I left her rather abruptly to return to the garrison and thought I would probably not see her again anyway.

I arrived exactly seven minutes late. By luck, a comrade from my division was on duty, and I got in without problems.

A few days later, I decided to visit Eliane at the address she had given me. She was there and looked happy to see me. We decided to take a bus, leave the noisy city and find a little restaurant in the country. We spent the entire afternoon talking, laughing, drinking wine and getting to know each other. I realized I had met a person as free-spirited as I was. We spoke about literature, quoted poems and watched the squirrels running up and down in the trees. Even the quiet moments between us felt comfortable.

We shared hopes and dreams. I found it unbelievable to be so open and free with someone, an enemy of my country, after all. It was the only uneasy feeling I had while being with her. We never spoke about the war and the German occupation of her country.

The day, much too quickly, came to an end and we had to return to the city. There, as we said goodbye, she suddenly took my face in her hands, stared into my eyes and said, "Come with me to Paris. I have a small flat where you could hide while I get you some French ID papers. I work and have enough savings for both of us for a while. You could start a new life and leave all this horror behind, the war will not go on forever."

I stared at her, not believing what I just heard. My thoughts were running wild. This could be a dream come true to get away from the war. Was this really what I wanted? All I needed to do was say yes and the rest could fall into place, I thought.

I could see she was really serious about it, but felt unable to make such a decision. Right or wrong, I took her in my arms and kissed her with passion as she returned my kiss. Then I did what I had to do. I turned from her and walked away. No! I ran as fast as I could, feeling her eyes on me the whole time. Before turning a street corner I slowed down to look back. There she stood under a street lamp in the distance, very still without giving any sign. Then, she turned slowly and walked away, becoming fuzzier, smaller and smaller, until she disappeared from my sight.

Had I then foreseen the future, and what life had in store for me, perhaps my decision would have been different. But, it is what it is, no one can change his destiny. One can deviate, but destiny is destiny. Even in these early days of my life, I believed that everything is written out for us and the wheel of life continuously turns, whether we want it or not.

5
MARCELINE

Two weeks went by with hard work during the day. I had little desire to leave the base on weekends. However, one sunny Sunday morning I decided to go for a walk, and my steps led me to the city.

As I arrived at the main town square, Place de La République, I ran into three comrades in the company of girls. They asked me why I was alone, and if I was too shy to find female companionship. Annoyed, I told them I was enjoying a stroll and was quite capable of finding company if and when I chose. They started laughing and mocking me.

Just then, as if by coincidence, a young girl happened to cross the street in our direction.

I don't know what came over me, but I was determined to show my comrades what I could do.

I smiled at them and told them to meet me in fifteen minutes at the corner tavern. If I came back without the girl, I would buy a bottle of champagne for all. If, on the other hand, I came back with this girl, the bottle would be on them. The bet was on. They laughed their heads off as I turned to follow the girl.

My unknown prey must have sensed something; she quickened her steps. I kept up with her and my first attempt to speak to her was unsuccessful, to say the least. I realized it would be harder than I thought. Time was running out. I did not want to lose this bet, and decided to approach her with the truth. I put on my saddest face, the one my mother could never resist, and hoped it would work with her. Almost out of breath, I told her my story.

"So," she said in almost perfect German. "It's all about a bottle of champagne?" She looked at her watch. "I don't have much time, but let's go and surprise your friends and have you win that bottle."

Three minutes before the time was up, we arrived at the café. The look on my comrades' faces was almost laughable. They were speechless. Champagne was ordered, and the conversation was pleasant. The young girl stayed longer than I had expected. She seemed to enjoy herself and would now and then look at me with interest. I have to admit that she was very attractive and made a good impression on me. I kind of hoped deep down that this little adventure might lead somewhere. She was of average height, perhaps five feet five, and had a slim figure, black wavy hair and brown eyes. Her name was Marceline. She looked to be about eighteen years old. Little was I to know that this young girl would someday be my wife. Sometimes it is best not to know what the future has in store for us.

This little adventure turned into a beautiful romance. We met most Sunday afternoons on my days off. I liked her more and more as we got to know each other better. I called her Mali to shorten her name and she nicknamed me Uli. Her fiery temperament suited mine very well.

We talked a lot and I told her about my life in Germany and my parents. She told me about her parents, who she said would kill her if they saw her in the company of a German soldier. I did not expect this to lead anywhere, it was just a nice way to spend my time off base. Also, she helped me, in time, to get a better command of the French language.

At that time, a new companion also came into my life. One evening, at the front of the barrack's gates, I found a lost German Shepherd puppy. He reminded me so much of the one I had lost, my Bubby. I tried to chase him away, but he hung on to me. I worried about keeping him and getting attached again, but his eyes begged for love.

I named him Prinz because of his good manners and refined taste in food. German Shepherd or not, there was no doubt he was French when it came to food. He was a fast learner and very disciplined. Dogs were allowed on the base, especially German Shepherds, who were favored by the military. We became very attached to one another and he loved Mali as well; therefore, we shared him. Every other week he would stay at her house, then with me on the base again. In no time, he knew the way from the barracks to her home and back.

Mali lived on the outskirts of Metz, in a little suburb called Sablon, on Gardner Strasse. It was a lovely community with quiet streets lined with birch trees and lovely little shops such as butchers, bakeries, shoemakers, etc.

Metz is the central city of Lorraine. A land with lush rolling wooded hills and meadows that is best known for its production of coal, iron, steel and white wines. Its closest neighbor, Alsace, is a big producer of grapes as well. Therefore, a vast array of white wine is produced in that region.

These two provinces have been fought over again and again in history. Lorraine and Alsace have been the chief subjects and victims of a long-standing conflict between Germany and France. Therefore, in those two regions, German and French are spoken fluently. Even to this day, many streets and shops still have German names.

Figure 3. Marceline Meyer, 1940

Mali had two sisters. One older, Cécile, and one younger, Georgette. They were part of our little secret rendezvous.

I guess Mali must have eventually told her parents she was seeing me. One day, I received a formal invitation to dinner from Mali's parents. I was very nervous about this meeting and dressed in civilian clothing. Contrary to what I expected, being German and at war with their country, I was well received. They asked a lot of questions about my family, my upbringing, why I joined the military, etc. I guess I must have passed the test with flying colors because I became a regular welcomed guest on the weekends. However, I always felt a certain reservation from her parents. Something I could easily understand and accept under the circumstances.

At least they were not against us seeing each other, and I made my best efforts to earn their trust.

I enjoyed having a family life of sorts.

As time went on, we fell deeply in love and I hoped my stay in Metz would go on for a while. I knew at any time I could be shipped out to the front lines again and kept my fingers crossed.

One day a friend of mine said he had seen Mali in town with another soldier. Jealousy swept in; I was in love for the first time. I tried to push it from my mind, but deep inside, I had a nagging feeling. Was this young girl playing around? I reasoned with myself, how could I mistrust her without any proof?

In January 1941, we became officially engaged and started making wedding plans. Her parents did not seem to be against it. I wished I could present her to my parents, and at the same time, I feared their reaction to this relationship.

Despite my military duties, it was the most beautiful time in my life. I couldn't wait for the weekends to be with her.

A few weeks later, my comrade mentioned once more that he had seen Mali in town in good company. Again, I tried not to pay attention to the rumor but asked Mali if there was any truth to it. She laughed innocently and said she had once or twice run into the brother of a friend of hers and they had coffee together. She became upset and told me I had no right to question her, she was free to come and go. Of course, she was right—how could I question her and not trust her?

News was spreading around the base and was confirmed by our Command Officer. We would be on the move to the front lines again very soon. No details were given as to when or where we would be deployed.

It had been so easy during these last few weeks to forget about the war and the fighting.

The news came as a shock. The time had come to face reality again. I was so in love, nothing else had seemed to matter, but now the forthcoming separation from my future bride lay heavy on my mind. Fourteen days later we received news that our departure would be on February 28, 1941, direction the Balkans. Will this damned war never end, will peace ever come?

It was difficult to announce the news to Mali but nothing could be done about it. The last few days were bittersweet. We tried not to talk about it, but a constant cloud hung over us.

6
THE KINDNESS OF A STRANGER

The day came when we stood with hundreds of soldiers at the departure gate of the train station in Metz, our materials already loaded. It was around midnight and our departure was to be at 2:30 a.m. Mali and I needed to get away from the noise and commotion. We found an empty train wagon where we stayed together for about an hour.

My dear Annita, if by chance these pages fall into your hands someday, know that this was more than likely the day you were conceived. Perhaps not at the best time in history, or in the most romantic environment, but with love. The goodbyes were very difficult. I held a crying Mali in my arms and had to be really strong for her. One last kiss and hug and I was on the train.

I can still see her standing there crying and waving as our transport train pulled out to take us once more toward an uncertain future.

I sat by the window of my compartment, gazing straight ahead and oblivious to what was going on around me. Only on the second day, while on train duty, did my sad mood pick up a little. I had to reason with myself and believe that I would return to Metz someday. The night was dark, and the speed of the train, the cold air and wind, brought some sense of hope again. I looked up at the sky; the moon was a bright crescent surrounded by stars. I wondered if Mali was seeing the same sky at that very moment.

I stubbed out my cigarette and decided I would survive all this. Someday, life would return to normal again. Someday all would be well, it had to be.

Forty-eight hours later, we arrived in Prague, the so-called Golden City. We stopped there only for a short time before continuing toward the Hungarian border. Two more days went by while passing through the dry barren countryside of Poland, with its famous draw wells, cow pastures, and poor peasants. Finally, exhausted, we arrived in the town of Kampolung in Romania. We stayed there for another couple of days to rest before boarding the train again for Bulgaria.

In Sofia, Bulgaria, we changed trains and headed to Greece. We reached the Greek border and had to go over a 1,300-meter icy pass, some of us on foot, in tanks or on horseback. We lost two tanks, some ammunition, a couple of horses, as well as a few lives. The road up was extremely treacherous and difficult. It was nighttime and we were crawling along the edges of steep cliffs, exhausted and in low spirits.

When we arrived in Salonicki, the Brits had begun to retreat and were moving south. The loss of our men was minimal so far, and we marched on toward the Gulf of Corinth. There was no time to think or even wonder if we would still be alive the next day. It was moment by moment.

Greek and British troops were assembled near Patras on the Gulf side for a counterattack. The slaughter was again unbelievable and more of our men lost their lives. Burned trucks, carcasses of military material and disemboweled tanks that looked like sardine cans made such a contrast with the beautiful landscape and the sun shining on white houses.

The first night there, I could not help but look at the bright stars over the sea again and wonder how my Mali was doing so far away. When would I hear from her? Would she forget me?

It took a few days to conquer Corinth and Patras. Our death toll was heavy but nothing compared to the terrible loss the Greeks and British troops suffered. I prefer not to recall the sight and smell of death all around us. I can only sincerely say I never intended to kill, but orders were orders and it was us against them, our lives against theirs. We were all humans, but we were enemies also.

The prisoners we took were worn out, dirty, and morally beaten. Their eyes reflected a loss of hope and the knowledge that they would never come out alive from this war one way or another.

How I wished those in high power, sitting smugly behind their desk, could have seen what we saw. They were the ones bringing the masses against each other and giving orders, orders to kill and slaughter, orders we had to obey.

It took only a few days to end the fighting. Greek and British soldiers who survived were made prisoners and sent to German war camps. The British forces, who managed to escape, went on further toward Africa. Greece was now in German hands and we could take a few days of very much needed R and R.

One evening, as I sat in a small café with other soldiers listening to Greek music and enjoying a drink, I saw a middle-aged man sitting in a corner at the opposite side of the room, sad looking and lost in his thoughts. At one point, our eyes met and I could not help but feel a deep sadness for him.

I don't know what prompted me to get up and walk over to his table. I asked in German if I could offer him a drink. To my surprise, in broken German, he thanked me politely but refused. I nodded politely as he got up to leave. Halfway to the door he turned around, looked at me and returned to the table. I ordered a couple of drinks. After a moment of silence, I introduced myself to him. He did not reciprocate but asked if I would accept a drink at his home. He lived only a short walk down the street. I accepted and followed him without a word down a dark and narrow alley. I realized it could be foul play, but something kept me going against my better judgment. A few minutes later, we arrived at a typical little Greek house that at one time must have been painted bright white, but now looked gray, shabby and badly in need of repair.

I entered with him and the contrast was surprising. The interior was glowing with soft candle lights, a warm fire was burning in a small fireplace, and the room, although poorly furnished, looked welcoming. He took out a bottle of ouzo, and poured two glasses. An old lady came out of a back room, said a few words to him, ignoring me totally, and left again.

As we sat by the fire he explained he had learned some German while studying engineering in Stuttgart, Germany, some years back as a young man. He spoke broken German but we could communicate. We toasted, but I felt very uneasy and out of place. How could this man be so kind to me? He was soft spoken as he told me his son had been killed recently by Germans, and his wife had passed away a couple of years earlier from an illness. He showed no hatred, just deep sadness and resignation. There sat a man in front of me who had lost a son my age, killed by my people, and was speaking to me, his enemy. He spoke without hatred, as if he had known me a long time. There was an instrument in a corner that resembled a guitar. He followed my gaze.

"It was my son's bouzouki," he said as his eyes filled with tears. He told me about his life, the hopes he once had, the loss of his wife and child. I told him about my life and family, how I had fallen in love with a French girl and how deeply I regretted what this war was all about. He seemed to understand and told me he had a close relationship with other members of his family in the village that kept him going. I realized the need he had to talk and share his feelings, and I felt honored it was with me.

I took leave of him a couple of hours later. He shook my hand in a strong grip and wished me luck and safety. I walked the streets for a long time, my heart terribly sad and heavy, thinking that no one would believe that such goodness still existed in those terrible times. I knew I would never see this man again, but he would forever leave an imprint on my heart, an imprint of kindness and forgiveness, a lesson of love.

7
RUSSIA

A month passed before mail arrived, a letter from my Mali. I had written several letters that had remained unanswered. Perhaps they had never reached their destination. My little Mali was writing that she was so terribly sad, worried and depressed and that she missed me. She was doing well and was pregnant. The news made me jump with joy and worry at the same time, but it gave me new hope again.

I could not believe I was to be a father. I managed to send a letter back immediately. Reassured her that I was safe, told her of my happiness, that someday we would be reunited and to stay strong. I would never have wanted her to know how terrible the past weeks had been and how uncertain the days ahead were. But now, more than ever, I had a reason to live and survive whatever was ahead of me.

Two weeks later, we boarded the transport train, again for an unknown destination. It soon became clear that we were headed back to Prague and from there to Budweis.

On the route, we stopped in Bratislava, Slovakia. The people there were welcoming and offered us beer and sandwiches. We stayed for twenty-four hours and pulled double shifts around the train. Balkan partisans were always ready to attack and sabotage German transport trains, and we had to be vigilant.

We moved on again the next morning. I could not have been happier with the knowledge that the return trip was bringing us closer to the homeland. I hoped that perhaps we would be given leave after this long period of fighting and traveling. The landscape again became familiar; apple trees were in bloom and in some places one could almost forget a war was going on. I was given a six-ton Mercedes and followed a column of eight other trucks headed for Prague to a military base to have the vehicles repaired. But all the garages in Prague had an overflow of work, so our trucks and cars had to be transported by train to Budweis.

Upon arrival, we reported immediately to High Command and were told we would be staying here at least two to three weeks before moving on again.

Budweis was a small and pleasant city. We took advantage of those few days of rest. The first night there, some of us found a cozy little bar and ended up having a few drinks too many.

It helped us forget the atrocities we had lived through and seen. We returned to the base later that night with our boots hanging from our shoulders, singing German songs at the top of our lungs, and little money left in our pockets.

The days went by, and soon we received news that some of our German troops had invaded Russia. Before we knew it the alarm rang in our division. We were all on our feet waiting for orders. We packed; transports and arms were ready. We were again aboard a military train riding through Poland into Russia. Off we were to another country to put our lives on the line once more. We endured exhaustion and our nerves were taut as we moved closer and closer to hell again.

Fights erupted on the train among the boys. They had to let off steam one way or another.

I could not help thinking of my little Mali, who was so looking forward to my homecoming, again postponed. Would I see her again? Would I know my child? Every day those were the same questions going around and around in my head.

While the train rolled on and on, I thought of my father. Russia 1914–1918, and now it was his son's turn twenty-some years later. How will it go this time? What did the future hold?

I had a deep feeling of oppression and gloom in my chest. None of us were prepared for what was ahead.

I looked out the train window to find even the smallest star, as I usually do, but it was a dark and cloudy night, like a warning of things to come. We kept on riding through the Polish countryside, and during some stops on the way, we talked to German soldiers who were headed in the same direction on different trains. Fear was in the heart of all. The endless, familiar fear we lived with, day in and day out.

Many miles lay ahead of us and there was lots of time to ponder and meditate as to what the future held. Several times I sat on the platform of our wagon and thought of the passing years. Two and a half years had gone by since this had started. How fast it all went, and how much had happened in that short time. I was a child one moment, then suddenly a soldier at war against France and the Eastern countries and now a father-to-be. I wasn't even twenty-one and felt old and tired. Many of my comrades had died, and who knew if in the coming days, the cool earth would cover me too. But what use is it to worry, it is all in God's hands anyway.

So many things were going through my head. Memories of days gone by. Vacationing by the sea with my parents, horseback riding through the countryside, my first glass of wine, running through the woods with friends and playing pranks, my first kiss. Peaceful and joyful were those days. Now it was horror, fear, and chaos. A voice pulled me from my reverie. We had twenty minutes left before arrival at the end station.

Once again, it is of no use to go into the details of what awaited us at the end of this trip.

We were dropped off just a few kilometers from the Russian border. I can only say we faced difficult, dark and horrible times, taking cover in muddy trenches with the whistling of bullets and grenades overhead, bombs exploding in the distance and screams from all directions.

It was no easy task running back and forth through empty Russian dirt roads and streets to get fuel and food for our camp. Our eyes were swollen from fatigue, dust and smoke.

Three weeks went by this way with our attack on Russia. Many of our men had died of diarrhea, diseases and lice infestation. Food rations were getting low, trucks were getting stuck in the melting ice and mud. It was getting more and more difficult to move on. Fatigue, cold and hunger were some of our biggest enemies.

Marshall Stalin's troops fought tough and mean. They were used to the Russian climate and conditions, but we still had the upper hand. Columns and columns of Russian prisoners walked by us going west. Their uniforms torn, some with no shoes, some with feet wrapped in cloth, but still they marched on toward a terrible future awaiting them at the hands of Germans. A few had the strength to sing Russian folklore songs, lamenting sad songs.

A young prisoner walking in a column, perhaps seventeen years old, passed by us one day and begged in German, "Please, Meine Herren, please, hungry." Several of them looked as if they had not eaten in days and were ready to collapse. I could not help it, and at the risk of getting shot by my own men, I reached into my breast pocket and pulled out a piece of stale black bread. The boy fell on his knees and tried to kiss my hands. Someone at my side spoke to him in Russian. The young boy explained that his parents were Ukrainians, and had fallen into Russian hands and been sent to Siberia. He and his brother enlisted for the front lines. His brother had been killed the very first day. I could only feel pity for this young boy as he marched on, head bent and chewing on the stale piece of bread. He had already witnessed so much tragedy at his young age and only God knew what was ahead for him. We were the ones who came into their country to take it over.

Germans, Russians, or any others who had died fighting, those deaths were in vain. Nothing had shortened or ended the war so far, and nothing would. I had lost hope totally.

Finally, our division was replaced by another one, and we were able to go back to base camp for a few days of much-needed rest. After the third day, we were sent toward the southern parts of Russia. The first defeat the Russians faced did in no way mean the end of the war. They still had strong forces in the northern and southern parts of Russia. We were now to move toward the sections of Dnipropetrovsk in Ukraine, Scherzon and Taganrog, toward the Black Sea.

Before our units moved on to new targets, another soldier and I received orders to go to the nearest town to retrieve ammunition. It was around midnight as we drove off. A pale moon came out to make the road a little more visible. My co-driver fell asleep next to me. As I came to the first road crossing I stopped, no signpost. They must have been removed on purpose. Three roads were branching off, and I could not turn on the headlights at the risk of giving away our position to the air raids. Calculating, I chose the road to the left, and after about twenty minutes of driving, an inferno broke out in the still night. A huge shock rocked the car and my head hit the steering wheel.

I felt around me for my gun but a powerful blast shook me again. I tried all I could to remain calm. What was happening? At first I could not hear or see anything. My ears were buzzing and we were in complete darkness. As I came to my senses and the smoke subsided a little, I saw in the moonlight my comrade's face; it was black as coal. By sheer luck, we were not wounded. We realized we were on Russian partisan ground and had hit a remnant of a mine. Thank God we hit it only with the right rear wheel. As quickly as possible, we grabbed our weapons and identity papers and ran toward what we hoped would be the next camp of German troops. Luck was with us. We announced ourselves to the commanding officer, who by radio was in contact with our division, and we were cleared to enter the camp.

We were given another car the next morning and returned to our camp with the needed ammunition and a road map.

On we moved again, heading south. We arrived after several hours of strenuous marching to the little town of Bobrinitz and spent the night there. Around 3:00 a.m. we awoke to the sounds of gunshots and found out that a band of Cossacks had ambushed us. Unbelievably strong and wild were these men on their horses, it was like watching a movie. After several hours of fighting we had the upper hand. Among the bodies of men and horses, we found several vodka bottles and before heading out again did some well-deserved celebrating and thirst quenching.

Our destination was reached by midafternoon, and we could rest and sleep for a little while. But again, around 2:00 a.m. we were pulled out of a deep sleep. The alarm rang all around us. "The Russians, the Russians." In no time we were up and ready; steel helmets and guns at hand, we took our spots to fight against dispersed Russian units trying to flee the southern borders. The fighting lasted until daybreak, as if all hell had broken loose. Our division suffered six deaths and fourteen were severely wounded. Dead Russian bodies were scattered all around, as well as many wounded.

We passed burning villages and fields, where women, children and the elderly left behind were eyeing us with fear. The poverty of these people was a sad sight. Most houses were nothing but mud huts. I marched on, chewing on a little stale bread and a raw onion.

It took another week to arrive in the southern regions of Russia. Nikolaiew and Odessa had also fallen into German hands. It was the same sight everywhere. Columns and columns of trucks, materials and men were moving on toward the front lines under the most difficult conditions.

Before reaching the harbor town of Tcherzon, we met with a group of Romanians fighting under Russian command. It took but a couple of hours to get the situation under control and continue on to Taganrog. No loss of lives on our side this time.

In Taganrog, we were able to get a few days of rest. We were close to the island of Crimea and the area was rather peaceful, no partisans in sight. It was a beautiful part of the country overlooking the Black Sea. At night with the full moon, one could almost forget a war was going on. I could not help again to think of Mali and wonder how she was doing. When would we see each other again? How was her pregnancy going? It was so frustrating to be without news of my loved ones.

One evening, a comrade and I took a walk through the streets of the little town of Taganrog with its small houses, poor but well kept. Through the small windows you could see walls decorated with calendars, pictures cut out from old magazines, some religious objects, icons and rough-looking furniture. We came upon a little wooden cottage of typical Russian style.

My comrade said, "Can you hear?" We stopped to listen and heard a soft, melodious young girl's voice singing to the notes of a balalaika.

We approached the cottage slowly, peeked through a small window and saw a cute young Russian girl sitting in a corner picking at her balalaika. Two women were peeling vegetables. This wonderful voice in the middle of war-torn Russia tore at my heart, as did the sight of a united family. I had a difficult time falling asleep that night. So many thoughts were going through my mind.

Back home we also sang cheerful songs on the accordion or harmonica, toasting and clinking big beer mugs. Someday . . . Someday again, . . . God willing.

8

THE LOSS OF HOPE

The next morning, to my greatest joy, there was mail from Mali, telling me she had received several of my letters all at once. Therefore, she knew I was now in Russia but was very worried for me. She had enclosed a photo of herself and I had a hard time recognizing her. She had changed into a beautiful woman, and my longing for her became even greater. I could see that her pregnancy became her. It gave her the glow women have when they are expecting. When! Oh! When will this nightmare end? When will I see her again?

Figure 4. Marceline Meyer, 1941

Above us, Russian warplanes made our lives hell and ground on our nerves day and night. Those little machines were fast and agile, like swallows. Day and night we aimed at them and they at us.

The pilots were daring and well trained; they kept coming back again and again. Around us was the Russian army with artillery fire covering them. We felt like we were in a witches' cauldron.

It was now September of the year 1941. The days were getting colder, and an icy wind was blowing in from the Black Sea. Our orders were to stay put and not to march on for the time being. Were we to spend winter in Russia? The famous Russian winters! I could not even imagine what it would be like. Already we wrapped our faces and feet with whatever cloth we could find to keep from freezing and slept body to body at night. We were ill-prepared and the Russian troops going westward made mincemeat out of Hitler's Panzer divisions. German uniforms and weapons were not designed for the brutal Russian winters, and it would not be long before Hitler's men would be completely overwhelmed. The soldiers of the Red Army were provided with shoes two sizes larger. With frost, the feet swell, and they had space to fill the shoes with straw or newspaper to prevent freezing.

The 4th and 5th Panzer divisions were losing one soldier every seven seconds, and contact with our other units was lost.

My health was not at its best. We all had lost a lot of weight, looked emaciated and had little desire to joke, laugh and even talk with one another. Food was becoming scarce, as were ammunition and cigarettes. Despair filled our hearts and morale was at its lowest. The continuous cold, blowing wind was grating on everyone's nerves.

The day came, however, when we received orders to return south. We could only obey those in High Command, sitting behind the safety of their desks, and abide by their rules. Kill and kill again and again; we became animals. Survival for us was all that mattered at this point, and again we marched on, never knowing what to expect next. We lost more men on the way, too weak and too beaten. Some even committed suicide. I kept moving, not looking behind in fear of losing my courage and ending my life.

It was October 2, 1941, the day before my twenty-first birthday. The news spread that we were surrounded by the Southern Russian Army. This was a big blow to us, but we were given the reassurance that German Reserve Army anti-tank divisions were on their way and would arrive anytime now to ensure our safety. I needed to believe it was true to keep my sanity.

I thought my birthday would never come to be anyway. All hope of someday seeing my loved ones again was a faraway dream at this point. The end was near for all of us and my child would never know its father. How can one explain the despair, the loss of hope in the midst of killings and carnage? I hit the lowest point in my life. Hunger was driving all of us crazy. The frozen ground offered no vegetation. Not even a single blade of grass. Even worms would have been a welcomed sight.

We kept our position two more days with no help on the way. Day after day, the thick smoke of combat engulfed us. I didn't feel well and came down with a severe onset of fever. I had to stay lying down inside a truck covered with filthy blankets, shivering uncontrollably, helmet on at all times and gun at my side. I felt too weak to do anything or even care. Some of my comrades would come by to bring me medicine and watery soup whenever they could.

On the third day, things got worse; the regiment medic diagnosed me with pneumonia. I was transported to the field medical unit a few kilometers away. What's the use, I thought. In a few days we would all be prisoners or killed anyway. My mental outlook had hit bottom. Being killed would be better than being held prisoner by the Russians. I could only imagine the atrocities they would put us through.

My transport, spent lying on a gurney, was infernal. The ride over mud tracks was rough, to say the least. Every move hurt. My head was splitting from fever and pain. My throat was parched. In my feverish state I could hear, from very far away, gunshots and bombs, but I really didn't care anymore. I closed my eyes, thinking that many of us would be gone before the sun would set.

Two days later, I regained consciousness and realized I was under a military medical tent. Many sick and wounded lay on gurneys or the bare floor next to me. The fever was still high, but I felt waves of hunger that were soon forgotten as heavy artillery fire hit us.

Everything is but a blur from that moment on. I remember screams and terrible chaos, being ordered to get up and put on a helmet. I stumbled on my weak legs and with the help of another soldier was dragged to what looked like a truck or ambulance. As the artillery fire came closer and louder, someone screamed. "Help me, help me!" I turned to see a soldier from our unit trying to lift a wounded comrade, pulling him from under the armpits. Someone took his feet. I saw that the wounded man was very young and bleeding from the mouth as his head rolled back and forth. They put him on a stretcher next to mine in the truck. I reached over to hold his hand. All I remember then was a huge explosion and being propelled into darkness. From that moment on, I have no recollections.

It was on the evening of October 7 that I regained consciousness again. A doctor was at my side, telling me to remain calm. I heard voices from far away. My eyes tried to focus on white walls and what appeared to be a very large room. As I moved, a terrible pain shot through my head. Slowly, I tried to lift my right arm to touch my head, but it was tied to the bed. I tried with my left arm and felt that my entire head and forehead were bandaged. The strong smell of chloroform and medicine hung all around. I could hear men moaning and screaming in pain as I passed out again. I don't know how long it was until my senses came back little by little. A nurse dressed in white came to my bed and put a hand on my arm. "How are you feeling?" My answer was, "Where am I?" I remembered having a high fever but no injuries. I was sure I was on my way to the big commando in the sky and it was surely an angel speaking to me.

She said I had a serious head injury. I had been hit by Russian artillery fire and brought here a few days ago with several others. She asked me to lay still. "What day is it?" I asked.

"October seventh," she answered. There were so many wounded around me. The noise and screams were unbearable. My head was throbbing and again I passed out blissfully.

A military doctor came again a day later to briefly check on me, and left without a word. It seemed as though no one had time for an explanation. I had no idea where I was and what was going on besides muffled gunfire in the distance and the screams of the wounded. In the coming days, my bandages were changed often, but I could not get a mirror to look at myself. The nurses were there to turn me from side to side every few hours and help with the use of a bedpan, which I hated, but I was too weak and unable to sit up by myself. The field hospital was filled to the max and there were only two doctors on duty, who took turns day and night. Flies were buzzing around my head and I didn't have the strength to chase them off. In my delirious state, I was imagining it was music.

War! Oh War! What horrors you bring . . .

A few more days went by. I gained strength little by little and found out our troops had pushed back the Russians. I wondered how many of my comrades who had continued fighting were safe or dead at this moment. I cannot say if it was my will to live or just luck, but each day I became stronger and stronger. I was able to get up with help and take a few small steps at first. Fifteen days later, I was told that my bed in the hospital was badly needed and I would be transferred soon. Several of us had been given a clean bill of health and, right or wrong, we had to make room for the daily onslaught of wounded coming in by the thousands.

While in the field hospital, I had become acquainted with another German soldier from southern Germany who had throat and arm wounds. He was fluent in the Russian language, and this would later come in very handy for both of us. We were loaded onto trucks and off we went, destination unknown.

The ride was certainly most uncomfortable. My head was still very painful and pounded with each move of the truck, and I had a hard time breathing. I thought the trip would never come to an end. One who has no knowledge of Russia and its landscape cannot imagine how far and wide this country is and how wearisome and unending it can be to travel through. And there was the constant danger of being attacked.

We were brought to the town of Dnipropetrovsk, where we would be treated at a German reserve hospital. On the way there we were stopped by a Russian police patrol. Although Russia was in German hands at this time, there were still some checkpoints and Russians who thought they were in command. This is where my new friend's Russian language was helpful. He never told me what he said, only that the less I knew the better it was. Anyway, we were allowed to move on after our truck was ransacked of all food and medicine.

Our travels lasted two more days. I was again getting weaker and weaker. No food, but we had a little water. My head wound and lingering pneumonia did not help the situation.

We finally arrived at our destination and I had to be carried in by stretcher, unable to take one step on my own. My breathing was labored. My head bandages had shifted and were caked with dried blood.

What a blessing it was to be put in a real bed with sheets. We were bathed and shaved, and despite the pain, I felt like a human being again. I can only remember sleeping for two days straight and waking up hungry. Then, I was told by the commanding surgeon that I needed cranial surgery.

After the surgical procedure I was told a steel plate had been inserted on the right side of my head. Again, it took days before I realized what had happened. I drifted in and out of consciousness. But I must move on with my story; there is not much to say about being in a hospital and recuperating.

About three weeks went by before I started feeling like a real human being, and strong enough to be allowed to take walks in the hospital park with the help of a cane. It was wonderful to be able to move on my own again, to be outdoors and smell fresh air. Every once in a while, sounds of falling bombs could be heard in the distance, but it was far away.

The day came when I was called to the administrative office. I figured I would be released, that my head wounds had healed sufficiently and I would be sent back to the front lines. My God, will I again have to face hell? Why had I not died?

The door opened and the lead doctor came in, greeted me briefly, and sat behind his desk with a smile on his face. I thought to myself, you can smile all right, you are giving me a clean bill of health only to send me back to face death again. Looking at me, he said, "You are well enough to travel and be sent to a garrison hospital in Prague where you will continue your recuperation. You have a very serious head injury and although the surgery was successful, you are not ready for any strenuous activity and need rehabilitation. It will take time to heal. You have post-traumatic shock and there may be times when you will have lapses of memory. This is nothing to be concerned about. In time, you will get back to your normal self."

Could this be true? I was not to be returning to the front lines? I could not believe my luck, if you can call it luck. I found out that my friend had received the same good news and we would be able to travel together to the same garrison hospital.

Early the next morning, we took our leave, headed to Krakow, Poland. It took several days by train to get to Krakow. We were slowed down many times due to weather or air raids.

I remember sleeping a lot, if you can call it sleeping in a seated position. There were many men on the train. Some had lost a leg or an arm and were going home for good; some wounded like us were sent to different garrison hospitals and some back to the front lines. When we arrived in Krakow, we were taken to the main hospital where we underwent examinations and had our medical papers reviewed.

Then, we were sent on further to a specialized hospital in Prague. I had but one hope, to get better, to be able to get leave to see my parents and Mali again. However, for the time being, it was still a faraway dream.

9
BERLIN

We arrived at the Prague hospital and were again bathed and cleaned and received brand-new beds and clothing, as well as uniforms. My head was examined and freshly bandaged. I was told the injury was healing well and was taken to a long room with rows and rows of beds filled with sick men. I was shown to my assigned bed and thought what a blessing a bed was as I lay on it before I drifted off into a deep sleep.

Ten days later, the sutures were removed from my head wound, and for the first time in a long time I saw myself in a mirror. A bald head half-hidden with plaster stared at me. I was skin and bones, with dark circles under the eyes and bruises. It was a ghost staring back at me. If Mali would have seen me, what a shock it would have been.

On November 14, 1941, a telegram was delivered. Mali had received the news of my hospitalization in Prague, but more importantly, she announced that little Annita came into this world the day before on November 13, 1941. I could not believe I was now a father, I had a child. All I could think of was that as soon as I was well, I would be released from the military, go back to France and get married.

A few days later, to my greatest joy, the hospital let me go out to town for a few hours. Some comrades and I went to a restaurant in Prague to celebrate my new fatherhood. We were a sight, some on crutches, some with missing limbs, some of us still in bandages, but there was a smile on every face. For some the war was over, for others there was no way of telling what the future held in store.

On December 18, 1941, I was released from the hospital with an indefinite leave of absence from my battalion. I was to be sent back to Berlin to my original barracks for the time being. My head wounds were still painful; the slightest noise was uncomfortable. Sometimes, I had difficulty remembering names or dates, but I was on the way to recovery.

The night before leaving, I and several others who also were released went into Prague to a little restaurant to celebrate our last night together. None of us was likely to ever see each other again. We made the most of it over good beer, cheers and well wishes.

I boarded the train to Berlin early the next morning for the long, slow trip home. Finally, I arrived at the familiar station of my hometown. I could only think of what life had been like those last few months. I never thought I would survive and see this place again. Here I was, not looking anything like the young man my parents would remember, but alive.

Ernest, my buddy from the Russian front, was traveling with me. He was assigned to another area of Germany where he would be stationed. We decided to have one last beer together. As we sat in the little café across from the train station, I could see he was lost in deep thought.

"Hans, what harm would it do if we open our orders carefully, see what they have in mind for us and reseal it?" I thought about it briefly and agreed. I should never have done it, the orders were very unfavorable for me.

I was given three weeks leave, then three months at the reserve battalion in Berlin to recuperate, and most depressing of all, after that I would be back to the front lines. I had thought of many scenarios but never to return to the hell of Russia. My comrade had received the same orders; he was returning within one month's time to the Russian front.

He lifted his beer glass and toasted mine. "Damnation, Hans, let's at least enjoy these few weeks. What will be will be." He drank it down in two gulps, slammed it on the table and ordered another one. I could not follow his thinking; it was the worst news.

We spent another couple of hours together drinking beer before parting, each to our new destinations. We hugged and wished each other the best of luck. The chances we would run into each other again were slim to none. I was sent to the Fields of Force division and he was to report to a Panzer Grenadier division. I watched him walk away. His shoulders hunched over as if carrying a very heavy load. He never looked back.

At the barracks, I met with a lot of young recruits who had just finished training and were soon to move on to their new positions. To them I was an old soldier. They were excited to hear about what was going on at the front lines and were full of questions. I did not want to scare those young sparrows who were just learning to fly, as I once did. I told them as gently as possible about life on the front lines, while still including the seriousness of it all. It will not be a vacation on an exotic island, I thought. Patience, young men, you will soon experience the Soviet Paradise. I spent four more days at the barracks to be debriefed.

The day before my leave was authorized, I received another bit of surprising news. The message came from the High Command Carrier. I was promoted to Corporal-Noncommissioned Officer. Included was the medal of Front Combatant. I could not even rejoice. What did these High Command pigs know about the life of a soldier on the front lines? For all I cared, they could keep their damned medals. Did they see their friends lying dead or blown up in the ice-cold tundra of Russia, covered in mud, calling for their mothers in a last breath?

They never even heard the sound of a bullet whistling past their ears.

My hatred for them was so strong I could scream. But, I had to keep my cool and play the game of the grateful soldier fighting for the Fatherland.

That same evening, my father called from his place of work. He seemed very excited. I told him I would be home the next day if all went well.

One can only imagine what a welcome it was. Mother could not stop crying and was wondering how I had come out alive from Russia and remarking on how skinny I looked. When I took my hat off and she saw the head wound, I thought she would faint. I could not tell them yet I was to return there again soon. I just said that my orders had not yet arrived. There was no use in spoiling the precious and short moments together.

Figure5. Annita's German Grand-parents, 1943

I stayed for three wonderful days with them, although it was bittersweet with the thought of my upcoming departure. They understood my need to go to France and see my baby girl for the first time. I did not tell Mali of my arrival; I wanted to surprise all of them. I left my parents with a terrible sadness in my heart, again with the same question: When would I see them again?

10
LITTLE ANNITA

When the train pulled into the station in Metz, France, it was the greatest feeling of joy to see this city again where I had been so happy. There was, however, much destruction; a lot of shops were closed or barricaded. I took a taxi to Sablon, the suburb where Mali lived. I could not get over how beautiful that little street still looked to me, despite the destruction, as the house of my beloved came into sight. Although there was a lot of damage there as well, I could only see beauty. So much had happened, so many thousands of miles later, and here I was again.

As the taxi approached, I became more and more nervous. I paid the driver and ran to the front door, pushed my finger on the doorbell, and ran up the stairs. It all went so fast that I cannot remember much of what followed. There stood my little Mali, her eyes wide open in disbelief. Without a word, we fell into each other's arms, hugging and hugging with tears running down our faces.

I heard her mother's voice asking from the kitchen who was at the door. Mali put a finger to her lips and I followed her inside.

Mother Meyer was at the stove, cooking, and Father Jacob was, as I always remembered him, sitting by the radio listening to the news while rolling a cigarette one-handed between his thumb and fingers. Mali's sister Georgette, who was eleven then, was sitting at the kitchen table doing what looked like schoolwork.

Father Jacob dropped his cigarette, and his eyes bulged as big as a crocodile's. "It's Uli," he said as he ran up to hug me. I had never felt so important in their eyes before. Mother Meyer came to hug me as well, and Georgette was jumping up and down.

Mali took my hand, motioned me to be quiet, and led me down the hallway to her bedroom. In a corner stood a little wooden crib painted white and covered in lace. I approached with shaking knees and there she was, my little Annita. Her green eyes were open and she stared at me as Mali spoke to her. "This is your Daddy." I took her very carefully in my arms, afraid to hurt her, she was so small, and the three of us locked in an embrace. Annita never uttered a sound, just kept her eyes on me. Her little head was covered with blond, reddish fuzz. It was a breathtaking moment for me.

After all the slaughter I had seen, there was this new precious little life, so full of promises for the future. Mali put her back in the crib and we went to the kitchen, where her mother had started baking a cake in my honor—and an honor it was, because flour, eggs and milk were hard to come by in those days. The rest of the day was spent answering question after question; it seemed to have no end. At last, night came, and I could have my Mali to myself.

The permits to marry had arrived from Germany. My future in-laws made all the preparations, and a few guests, mostly family members, had been invited to the wedding. Two days later we went to the Metz city hall with our papers in hand, both very emotional.

However, bad news was in store for us. The mayor informed us that the provinces of Alsace and Lorraine did not recognize a union between a German and a French person without a special permit from both countries, which could take several weeks. We would have to be married first in my home city of Berlin, then bring back the marriage certificate and permit, and only then could we have a second civilian ceremony in France. We were totally demoralized. Everything was ready for the wedding that day; food and guests had arrived. I turned the city upside down that morning to find someone to marry us, but to no avail.

We celebrated our union anyway, as best we could under the circumstances. For we could not let the food and preparations go to waste. Never had I dreamed of such a wedding, not even in my wildest dreams.

Three days later, I boarded the train to Berlin with Mali.

It took only a couple of days to get the paperwork and be married in a civil ceremony in Berlin on March 17, 1942. We received the necessary documents to be married again under French laws: documents allowing a German soldier to marry a French citizen in war times. We had a family dinner at a small restaurant with my parents that evening. Mali got to know my family and it seemed to go very well.

There was no wedding reception or honeymoon. The very next day, we took the train back to Metz, France, for our civil ceremony. We were now legitimate in both countries, and Annita had dual citizenship.

We had a few more beautiful days in Metz before I had to report back to Berlin. My leave was over and it was time to say goodbye again. The eternal saga of my life.

Mali took me to the Metz train station. I can only say that the goodbyes were hard again. I had no clue when I would return or if there would be a next time for us. I held Annita in my arms, and as her little fingers wrapped around my thumb, tears filled my eyes. When would I hold my child again and see my wife? The train pulled out of the station. All I could see through blurred eyes was Mali crying and waving with our child in her arms.

11
BREATH OF FRESH AIR

As I sat there again on a train, I thought how trains and goodbyes had become a part of my life. I could only imagine what was ahead. I did not feel well, my head was pounding and I still had difficulty breathing. I figured it was from all the emotional turmoil and stress of the last few days.

I arrived later that evening in Berlin with a fever and a severe headache. After being examined by a military doctor, I was diagnosed with acute asthma and, again, was to stay at the base hospital for several days.

The chief doctor explained that the conditions and the harsh life of the front lines, the exposure to smoke inhalation, the weather and the lack of proper nutrition could be the cause for asthma. Along with the combination of severe head injuries and major surgical procedures, I probably would no longer be fit for active duty.

On one hand, my joy was great; on the other hand, asthma is a terrible disease. The feeling is as if someone holds a pillow over your face and crushes your chest to smother you. Sadly, it was to be little Annita's lot as well. She was diagnosed with the disease at the age of two.

Several weeks were spent at the military hospital. My parents visited almost daily. Most of my time was devoted to writing and poetry. There was little else for me to do. I sent many letters and poems to Mali and often wondered why she did not answer as often as I wished. Although my love for her was strong, I started to question the lack of news and wondered if her loyalty to me was as strong as mine was to her. I told myself that being cooped up, sick and alone made me selfish. She was now a young mother, and had a full-time job and other things on her mind.

One day I was given the news by the hospital director of my transfer to a sanatorium in Austria to recuperate for a few months. This was great news. Perhaps the war was behind me now and I could make plans for the future with a family life.

I arrived in Bichlbach, Austria. What a beautiful sight—the magnificent mountain range capped in snow with the traditional chalets, the meadows, the peace, the quiet. I arrived at a beautiful wooden lodge, flowers blooming at every window, and was taken to a small but comfortable room. There was a balcony overlooking the most beautiful views of the forest, meadows and mountains. Sheep, goats, and cows surrounded the property. The air felt blissfully clean and clear. My God, I thought, life could not get any better.

A couple of days after my arrival, I wrote a letter to Mali and enclosed some money for her and Annita to come visit me in Austria. What could be nicer than being together in this beautiful environment, untouched by war?

A few days later, I received a response telling me she had no time for such fantasies. She had Annita to take care of, as well as helping her mother with the household chores and working her new full-time job, and she thanked me for the money. I was very disappointed, to say the least; her letter was so formal and lacked feeling.

Day after day, my health improved and I was feeling stronger. Winter arrived, and I was allowed to go out for walks and even try short cross-country ski trips, which I did for the first time in my life. How beautiful it was, gliding in the sparkling snow through the woods. The first day out, I was to be back at the sanatorium for lunch, but got turned around and found myself lost by late morning.

By sheer luck, I met another skier, a woman to whom I explained my predicament. She laughed and told me to follow her, which I did with relief. Her parents owned a small tavern in the village. She invited me to have lunch with her.

She was about twenty-three years old. Her name was Lehni, and we spent the afternoon together laughing and talking. I had difficulties with the Austrian dialect but we understood each other anyway. We made a date to go skiing a few days later, and she helped me discover the most beautiful landscapes and places I could never have found by myself.

I felt a little guilty thinking that if my wife had come to visit, I would never have known this beautiful country as I was discovering it now.

I had never seen mountains as tall and majestic as those. The air was so pristine, I could not get enough of it. Lehni was an accomplished skier, and to my shame I could not keep up with her, which made her laugh and laugh at the top of her lungs. As stubborn as I was, I did all I could to get better, and once, to my greatest joy, I managed to get ahead of her. I think she might have done it on purpose, although she denied it.

We would glide for hours and hours and I never felt any fatigue. We crossed deer and antelopes. Animals I had never seen in my life. Could things get any better? In a selfish sense, I was almost happy Mali did not come. A few days later, Lehni told me she was returning to Munich to the university she attended and where she was studying medicine. We said our goodbyes. I told her how grateful I was for this short friendship, the time she spent teaching me to ski, and the beauty I had discovered in those mountains, and I promised her not to get lost again.

A couple of weeks later, I was released from the sanatorium with new orders. "Suitable for recruitment troops to another sector of Berlin, light office duty."

I went to the head doctor and told him I felt fit for something more challenging than light office duty. Could he not write a letter to High Command telling them that I was suitable for more than office duties? He told me there was nothing he could do about it and that it was not in his hands, orders are orders.

I should've been grateful not to have to go back to the front lines. As I was ready to take my leave from the doctor, the phone rang, and he motioned me to wait. I heard him say on the phone, "Now, tell me where in this village or hospital could I find a mechanic?" He hung up, shaking his head. I stood up and said, "I am a mechanic." He stared at me for a moment. "Herr Bosse, what was your specialty on the front lines?" Without flinching, I answered, "I was trained as an Elite fighter, and mechanic." He looked at me skeptically, picked up the phone, dialed and said to whoever was on the other end, "I think I found someone." Then, hung up and turned to me.

"I will get in touch with your commander in Berlin and see if we can have your orders changed. Since you are no longer suitable for duty on the front lines, you could be of use here. There is no guarantee it will work, but we can give it a try." I had to contain myself and hold back from beaming with joy. I knew very little about mechanical work, but had done some necessary repairs on the front lines. I knew I could learn fast if I put my mind to it.

To my joy the orders were accepted. I started my new job and hoped I would be successful at it. My parents visited as often as they could. Frankfurt/Oder was only about 200 kilometers away. I asked my father to bring some books on mechanic studies; it helped a lot.

I also received news from Metz on a regular basis and photos of Annita. She was changing so fast that I felt sad to miss those important moments that would never come back. However, in Metz, things were not going very well with Mali. She wrote she had issues with her parents and it was getting harder and harder to live at home. Things were not as she had expected.
She did not have enough money to move out on her own with the baby and was most unhappy.
I was away, not able to be a real husband or father, she complained, and she felt abandoned.
This news troubled me. After a few days, I spoke to the head doctor again, told him my predicament and that I needed to get back to Berlin, even if it meant holding a desk job at this point. It was the last thing I wanted to do, but I figured that once there, I could bring Mali and Annita to Berlin. He shook his head, but agreed to contact my commander again. Orders came two weeks later to have me transferred back. I was to report to High Command and start my new duties immediately as Assistant to an Obersturmführer.

My morale was low, my family was unhappy and I had a job I hated sitting behind a desk.
I decided to be firm and ask Mali to come to Berlin with Annita. She could find a job and my parents would take care of the baby during the day. At least we would be together on the weekends and I could see my child on a regular basis.
To my surprise, she accepted, and no more than a week later I picked them up at the Berlin train station. Annita had changed and grown a lot since I last saw her. We drove to my parents, where they would stay until Mali secured a job. I was again happy as I had my family nearby.

Mali found a job as a housekeeper for a wealthy family who ran a textile business in Berlin. Her salary included lodging, food, and every other weekend off to go back to Frankfurt to be with Annita. My parents were happy and became more and more attached to the baby. Things were finally working out, as far as I was concerned. I could see Mali during the week and spend weekends with my family in Frankfurt.

Again dark clouds loomed on the horizon. I received a call one day from Mali's employers. Could I come and meet with them at my earliest convenience? I got authorization the next day to leave the base and meet with Mali's employers.

When I arrived, my wife was not present and I was told she was in her bedroom. They wanted to speak with me privately and explained a gold bracelet was missing and could not be found.

"We do not want to accuse your wife, but we have the feeling she is not telling us the truth."

I was speechless and asked if I could see her.

I knocked on her bedroom door and, not getting a response, walked in. Mali was sitting on the bed and did not look up. I asked her what she knew about the bracelet. All she would say was that she was falsely accused and started crying.

Why did I not believe her? I almost took the room apart but could not find anything. What I found strange was that she would not move off the bed. I asked her to get up, but she refused.

I was now getting angry and confused. I pulled her up, grabbed the bed covers, pulled the sheets off and turned the mattress over, and there was the bracelet! My God, my wife, a thief?

I ran downstairs to return the bracelet, and was told that my wife had fifteen minutes to collect her belongings and get out of the house. That same evening I took her by train to my parents. I could not tell them what had happened and just explained that she was no longer needed at her job. There was no problem for them to take Mali in while she looked for another position.

On the return trip to the base, I was deeply lost in thought. I remembered that Mali had once lost her job at a theater in Metz where she worked as a cashier. I never knew the reason. Now, mistrust really filled my mind.

I went home to my parents as often as I had leave from the base. My biggest joy was to spend time with Annita. Mali, however, became more and more difficult to live with. She told me she wanted to go back to Metz and could no longer stand living here with my parents, being told what to do or not to do. I firmly told her that I was not going to hold her back, but Annita would stay here with my parents. She seemed surprised and agreed to try harder to get along with her in-laws and look for work. For a short while, things seemed to return to normal, and being in love with my wife, I put everything behind me and tried to forget.

As usual, my life seemed to attract clouds, and again they popped up. My health once more took a turn for the worse. Asthma attack after attack left me weaker and weaker, to the point where I was again hospitalized. This time in my hometown of Frankfurt near my family. The attacks were due, according to the doctor, to mental stress and a very severe nervous condition. Rest was all they could recommend, and as little stress as possible. My wife, little Annita, and my parents came to see me regularly. Everything seemed to go well for the time being. I was released ten days later and sent back to my command in Berlin.

12
1942

It was early winter 1942 when my mother came to visit me at my base office. My father had not been able to take leave from his job and she did not want my wife to know she had come to see me. She seemed extremely upset and I had to do my best to calm her down.

"Hans, I came to tell you that your wife is cheating on you. The neighbors are talking. She has been seen many times with other soldiers." Again, shock and mistrust hit me. Would I ever find peace in this marriage?

I decided to find out for myself, and the next weekend I took a fast train to Frankfurt. Spying on her made me uneasy and did not come to any results. I thought this was childish on my part anyway. I knew that my wife had made friends with the wife of a comrade of mine, and I went to see Erna. As I explained my suspicions to her, she shook her head and sadly confirmed that my wife was stepping out on me. I was now totally enraged and had to get myself under control before I confronted Mali. The rest of the week, I did a lot of drinking and planning.

The following weekend, I visited Mali at my parent's house and acted as if nothing were wrong. Later, after dinner, I went through her purse and found a letter posted from Berlin, confirming she was having an affair with a man by the name of Verner. But this Verner was not the only one, as I was to find out—there were several other names and addresses in a little notebook.

Now all hell broke loose inside of me. I ran back to the dining room, grabbed her by the arm in front of my stunned parents, and pulled her into our bedroom. I told her I knew everything and had proof. She got angry and called me a liar, a dirty German, and said that my parents had set me up against her. I lost all reason and grabbed for the pistol at my side. Just in time, the door flung open and my father ran to me, took the gun out of my hand, pushed me against the wall and slapped my face hard. I ran out of the room, left the house, and took the next train back to Berlin.

The following day, Father called to tell me that my wife wanted to return to France. He said they had refused to let Annita go with her and asked me to get home as soon as I could.

Again, I had to explain the situation to my boss, who thankfully let me go.

When I arrived home, Mali ran into my arms sobbing. We talked and she admitted having made acquaintances in Berlin and in Frankfurt because she was so lonely and far from her family and friends. She begged for my forgiveness and swore that it would never happen again.

I melted and gave in. My God! Can love be so blind?

She asked me to find her an apartment in Frankfurt, as she could not go on living with my parents. I agreed, and we set off to find new lodgings and were lucky to find a small flat I could afford. Mali was happy to finally have a place of her own to raise our child by herself.

Back at the barracks, I spent many evenings drinking one bottle of beer after another, uneasy and wondering if I could ever trust her again. I could only spend my weekends with her and during the week could not control her comings and goings. I just had to trust her, what else could I do? She was the perfect wife when I visited, and I blamed myself for not trusting her.

Why did I love her so much? It would be so much easier to let her go and send her back to France. At times, I thought she was the devil in disguise, but I loved her and could not let go.

My parents kept begging me to send her back to France, that the child could stay with them and that my life and health would only get better. I was heading for trouble, my father said. But I could not accept their advice and stubbornly believed that she would change and we could have a normal life.

A few more weeks went by and although my mistrust was great, we still had wonderful moments together when I went home to her on weekends. I started believing she had changed, but it did not last very long. We have an old saying in German: "Once the cat strays, it always will." And this time I caught her in the act.

A friend of mine from the military base had concert tickets but got sick at the last moment. He asked if I would be interested in going to the concert with a friend so the tickets would not be wasted. Being an opera lover, I was more than delighted and found a comrade to accompany me.

As I sat in a small loggia with my comrade and two couples, who were unknown to me, I saw a couple enter, three loggias down. My God! Could this be possible? My wife with a High Command officer?

She was supposed to be in Frankfurt with Annita; my parents did not tell me she would be in Berlin. And what was that fur coat she was wearing? The officer leaned over and kissed Mali full on the lips; both were laughing. Was I dreaming? Was this really happening? Rage took over and I started to get off my chair, but sat down again. He was a high-ranked officer and confronting him could get me in trouble; perhaps I would even be court-martialed if I did. My anger was so out of control that all I could do for my sake was leave the theater. I explained to my comrade that I wasn't feeling well and went back to the base.

I arrived at the barracks and got drunk that night. I had to wait a full week before getting time off to take the train to Frankfurt. This drove me crazy. Meanwhile, I called my father, told him this was the end, she was going back to France and Annita would stay here in Germany.

He informed me that he had researched French and German laws and found out I could not keep my daughter in Germany. The mother had the right to take her back to her country. Annita was born in France, even if she had dual nationalities. No law would be on my side.

The following weekend, I took the train to Frankfurt. My rage was very much alive. I tried my best to remain calm.

I stormed into the apartment. She came to me smiling. I slapped her full force in the face, told her to pack her bags and go back to France. I felt terrible to have lost control again and been physical with her. Of course, she denied having been to Berlin. It must have been someone who resembled her; she did not own any fur coat and told me to check her closets if I didn't believe her. I poured out my hate at her, grabbed a blanket, covered Annita and ran down the stairs with her. I could hear Mali crying and screaming, but my mind was made up.

I took Annita to my parents, and there I totally broke down. Father calmly told me that Annita would have to go back to her mother, there was nothing to do about it. I could go to jail if I took the child from her and would only get in trouble with the military law and the judicial system.

"How could I have been so blind? How could I have made such a mess of my life?" Many emotions ran through my head. Shame, stupidity, and so much anger.

I returned to the apartment where Mali lived. She was gone, and so were her belongings.

I ran to the train station but could not find her anywhere. No trains had left for France in the last five hours. Did she call her lover to pick her up?

Two days later, the military police came to my parents' home and took Annita to return her to her mother. Father Meyer had come from France and talked with my parents; of course, they could only find him right. Their meeting was amiable, and Father Meyer could only agree that his daughter had always been a problem for the family.

Mali probably had help from the famous Verner. There was nothing for me to do. I was in Berlin, and I never even had a chance to kiss my daughter goodbye one last time. It was the end of the year 1942, and my little one was only a year old.

13
DO YOUR JOB

Christmas came, and Hitler was heavily involved in World War II. How were we to come out of this terrible conflict that was getting worse by the day? Before I knew it, 1943 made its entrance. I was staying at my parents' and got very drunk that New Year's night with thoughts of my wife, my child and the mess I was in. Oh! Yes, I felt very sorry for myself.

One evening in July 1943, as I left my office on the base, to my utter surprise there stood my wife. She was by herself; Annita had stayed with her grandparents in France. She wanted to talk.

We spent the night in her hotel room, talking about everything for hours over several glasses of wine. Big mistake on my part. She seemed so sincere when she told me she had thought things over and asked for another chance. She would be the best wife and mother, if only I could forgive her. So much mistrust was in my heart, how could I ever forgive and forget? I missed my little daughter and would do anything to have a family life, but was this the right thing to do? I felt like a puppet pulled in all directions. I stood firm and told her to go back to Metz and to give me time to think things over.

She hung her arms around my neck, crying and kissing me. My weakness gave in as usual, and we spent the night together.

The next morning, I took her to the train station and told her that I would do what was right, but for now I could not decide and needed more time. We promised to write each other, and she agreed to wait and see what the future would bring. This war, I thought! Everything depended on it!

I was again at a low point in my life and requested an appointment with my commander.

I told him I felt fit to be assigned to the front lines again. My request was, of course, denied due to my head injuries and overall health. But I was given a transfer to a Reserve Commando in Stettin, Pomerania. I was not to be there very long though; in November 1943, I became ill again and was sent back to a hospital in Berlin.

I recuperated enough to be transferred from Berlin to a small military hospital on the edge of the Baltic Sea. There I was assigned a desk job again. I so loved those damned desk jobs. However, it was heavenly there; the fresh air of the sea, the beautiful untouched landscape revived me again. I spent many evenings watching the sunset and could not help thinking of my wife and Annita. Why could this woman not be true to me? What possessed her? Why could I not get her out of my head? I knew deep inside I could and would never trust her and that I needed to close this chapter of my life and move on. Sadly, I felt caught in a web.

Many times I looked across the sea, at Sweden, a land untouched by Hitler. Could one go there, live in peace and forget everything?

My new orders came. I was definitively to remain on office duty due to my failing health, and was assured that Hitler needed me just as much in the office as on the front lines.

Then came another big shock. I received news from Mali that she was four months pregnant. Annita was about two years old then. Oh, my God! I was to be a father again? I didn't even know my first child very well; how could I be father to a second child? All kinds of thoughts ran through my mind. Was this my child? Yes, we had been together the

Figure6. Marceline (Mali) and Annita end of 1943

last time she came to see me in Berlin last July. Did this new pregnancy change my wife's character? Would she now be the wife I needed, the mother to my children? She suggested for me to try to be transferred back to France again, wanted me close to her and the children. She was tired of having a long-distance marriage. However, this was out of my hands; we were at war, and I had no choice but to obey my superiors and follow their orders.

All the same, I asked for a transfer duty to Metz, France, and was put on a waiting list. Finally, in February 1944, an opening came up in the administrative section of a garrison in Metz. I received the assignment with a heavy sigh; I really did not look forward to going back to Metz this time. I took the long train ride back from the Baltic to Metz once more.

All along the way, the signs of war became more and more visible. Burning farmhouses, dead cattle in the fields, blown-up tanks covered in mud, lines and lines of wounded and exhausted people begging for food, and the stench of death everywhere. Looking out at this terrifying landscape, I thought that not so very long ago, I was in that same situation, thinking that death was easier than living.

Now I was heading back to France once more and I had no idea what the situation there would be. Mali had assured me she felt safe there for the time being, despite the bombings and nightly raids going on in Metz.

I arrived in Metz and immediately reported to my post commanding officer. This time, there was no joy in me to see the city again.

I had heard that Chief Taubert was not an easy man to get along with. I entered his office with some anxiety. A skinny man sat rigidly at his desk working on a pile of papers, ignoring my presence. I stayed at least two minutes at attention, which gave me plenty of time to observe him. I felt more and more uneasy as time went on. At last, without speaking, he lifted his head and looked at me, tapping his ink pen loudly on the desk. His little beady eyes behind round-framed glassed were piercing like ice as he looked me over from head to toe with contempt.

"At ease Corporal Bosse." His tone of voice was filled with irony as he picked up a folder and said, "I see from your report that you had health concerns in the past. The Reich needs strong able-bodied men. No more vacation at this garrison, you had it a little too easy.

Your duties will be to report to me, and I will need you at least eighteen hours a day. You have twenty-four hours to get settled."

He smirked, looked back at his documents as if I did not exist and said, "Dismissed." I saluted, clicked my heels, and turned to the door to do as he said.

"And do remember, Jews have no value, they are intolerable pests for Germany. Do your job."

I left his office with a sick feeling—what did I get into? I checked into my barracks, found my sleeping bunk, pushed my bag under the bed, and immediately was on my way to Mali's home.

I passed the Cathedral St. Etienne dating from the 11th century and saw the left wing had been destroyed by bombs. Other buildings had suffered heavy damage as well; this once beautiful city did not look like anything I remembered.

I arrived at Mali's after taking many detours in order not to be spotted. My in-laws were relatively friendly and Mali acted surprisingly loving. I filled them in on the latest happenings and told Mali that my duties would leave me very little time to see her, which didn't seem to make much of an impression on her. Our second child was due in a couple of months. She was not at her best in that condition and looked weary.

I asked to see Annita, who was taking a nap. We went to wake her up. When she saw me, she turned screaming to her mother and wanted nothing to do with me. I figured she had not seen me in a long time and probably did not recognize me. But the coming days did nothing to change the situation; she wanted nothing to do with me. I decided to give her time, but in the days ahead nothing changed. When I tried to get close to her, she would fight me and scream her head off.

My job turned out not to be as bad as expected. Although the hours were long sitting at a desk and running errands, it gave me time to correspond with my parents and even do some writing of my own, which was a treat.

I saw Taubert very little and mostly reported to his private secretary, which suited me fine.

Then the news came that German troops were retreating in some areas of Russia and that Germany was getting heavily bombed. American troops were moving in closer and closer.

I'd had no news of my parents for the last few weeks, and my worries began to grow. I wondered if this was the beginning of the end, and where was the victory Hitler had promised?

14
RETURNING TO FRANCE

As the days went by I sensed more and more uneasiness with my in-laws. At first I put it down to the stress everyone was going through. The dangers of bombings increased. Each day or night, they spent many hours hiding in the cellar as raids went on and on, and the area was heavily bombed. Everyone was on edge and nerves were raw with fear. My second child, a girl named Elvira, was born on April 14, 1944.

It was now June 1944, and American troops had landed on the beaches of Normandy. They would soon make their way toward Germany. Everyone in Lorraine was in danger.

My in-laws were making it very clear that I was more and more an unwelcome guest, an enemy of their country, a murderer, as I overheard them call me sometimes. I tried to provide them with as much food as I could and milk for the children. I knew times were tough for all of them and me as well.

The children were driving them crazy and it was clear I needed to find an apartment for my family. I visited Mali only on the weekends, and even that became very uncomfortable most of the time. Mali was very difficult to get along with. She had no freedom, had to be with the children twenty-four hours a day. Constant bickering with her parents drove her crazy, and Elvira was a colicky baby who cried from morning to night. The situation for Mali was unbearable, and she wanted me to do something about it.

I also felt that my in-laws were turning Annita against me. She only wanted her mother or grandmother, nothing to do with me. I had no right to discipline her or voice my opinion when I was present. This situation was becoming unbearable for me too. What was I doing here?

We had an air raid warning at the base one evening and were told that American troops were heading toward Lorraine and Alsace; heavy bombing and fighting were expected. I was able to provide my in-laws, wife, and children with gas masks. It was getting worse by the day, and more dangerous all the time.

We did not have to wait very long before the first heavy bombing raid started over our military base, as well as at the Metz train station, which cut off all communication. My in-laws lived very near the station, and I was terrified for all of them. I asked my supervisor to allow me a couple of hours of leave one evening to check on them and was able to borrow a motorcycle.

As fast as I could, I drove to their house.

The house was untouched. I ran up the stairs. Mali, the children and my in-laws were safe, sitting in the darkened kitchen. My in-laws looked at me with contempt and said: "We are fine, the Americans know what they are doing. You, and the likes of you, are going to get what you deserve. That coward Hitler is retreating." Mali, without a word or gesture, let me go back to the base. I never felt so dejected and lonely.

In the days to come, we were bombed heavily several more times, but nothing as serious as what Germany was going through. I knew the time was close and it would get very nasty in the days to come.

In the early summer of 1944, I was sent on a special mission to Paris to pick up military documents and get them back to Berlin. Paris was a beautiful city and I wished I could have seen this city under different circumstances. I had two days to spend wandering the streets and was impressed by the monuments and the architecture, and most amazed at the Eiffel Tower.

I even found myself wondering if I would run into Eliane, the girl I had met in Metz before Mali. I spent time at sidewalk cafés relaxing over beer or wine and sometimes a cup of espresso. I felt I had a lot to learn about French culture. It was a fascinating city. Although blackout rang every night at 8:00 p.m., high-ranked officers with French girls on their arms would head for the nightclubs.

I rejoiced at the thought of seeing Berlin again soon and hoped to get some time to see my parents as well. I had found out they were doing well as of the latest news I had received a month earlier.

When I arrived, I was astonished at the sight of Berlin; it was a disaster. The city had suffered heavy damage from the bombs. Thousands of people were leaving town by cars, bicycles or on foot, carrying heavy luggage.

My first duty was to deliver the documents to a firm on the outskirts of Berlin by the name of Elektro-Kaun. There I was told it would take two or three days before I could return to Metz with new documents. I had no idea what those documents were about, nor did I care. I had to see my parents, and as soon as I could, I called them in Frankfurt. There was no way for me to get to them. No trains were going to Frankfurt. Rails and roads were cut off. Russians were on the east side, Americans were moving in from the west.

When I connected with them on the phone, after a long delay, they reassured me that all was well. My father sounded tired and told me he was sure the war was lost for Germany. They were, however, more worried for me. I knew he was right, the war was lost, even if the fighting was still going on.

I cannot begin to explain the feelings running through my mind. I was the father of two children, married to a foreigner, a woman in whose love I could not trust, with the loss of the war in sight and my parents blocked on the east side of Berlin with the Russians advancing.

As I was deep in my somber thoughts, the air raid alarm came on. I had just enough time to grab my coat and run to an underground shelter as the bombs started falling. This went on all night, as it usually did. The next morning, the documents I was to return with to France were ready.

After another long train ride through desolate countryside, I arrived in Metz in the early evening and went straight to my wife's home. Again, it was the same cold reception. Annita wanted nothing to do with me, and I noticed how little Elvira seemed somewhat left to herself. Mali did not want to breastfeed her anymore, claiming that Elvira cried no matter what. Cow's milk would have to do.

I used every minute of my time off base to look for an apartment rental, hoping that my wife, no longer under her mother's influence, would change and things could be much better between us. I found a small place, with one bedroom, a kitchen and a bath. At first, Mali was not happy with the thought of moving to such a small apartment with no extra bedroom for the children. I pointed out that it was located in the center of town within walking distance from her parents, which would make it easy for her to go to and from and visit her parents as often as she liked. And it was all I could afford for the time being.

She finally gave in and I moved them into the apartment. I could only stay with them every other weekend, which again was cause for arguments. If it had not been for the constant air raids and bombs falling, I could almost believe that some happiness had returned between us. However, a barrier had also grown; the trust was no longer the same.

My constant thoughts were on how this war would end—was Hitler going to give up and call us back, or would the Allies get us? How wonderful it would be to return to Germany with my wife and children, be around my parents again and find a good-paying job.

15
LIBERATION BEGINS

In September 1944, I was dispatched to Berlin again to receive an unexpected promotion. However, the situation there was rapidly deteriorating. As I arrived at the Berlin main station around 10:30 p.m., the air raid siren came on. More than a hundred American airplanes dropped bombs nonstop for over an hour. I found myself with civilians and military personnel in a bomb shelter under the train station.

When the air raid was over, we realized we were buried under rubble and searched for a way out. No one seemed hurt or wounded. Next to me sat an elderly couple; the woman was holding her husband in her arms and rocking him. She looked up at me and asked if I could please help her. Her husband was not moving. I felt his pulse, tried to find a heartbeat, but quickly realized he was dead, probably of a heart attack.

All able men and strong women started digging with their hands for an exit. It took three hours to finally find a way out. To our horror, Berlin was on fire. Flames were shooting up left and right, smoke and screams all around us. It was a terrible sight. I walked and walked among rubble, smoldering ashes, bodies, children screaming and people in shock.

Finally, I found shelter at the entrance of what once was a hotel, now in ruins. I sat down and let the tears fall until I fell into a slumber despite the cold, noise and smoke. This was once my beloved city. The beauty of the avenues, the shops and cafés, the parks, all in flames, all gone in such a short time.

I woke up cold and shivering at the first light of dawn, ashes flying everywhere and sirens blasting. It took me some time to find the way to the command base, where a dozen other soldiers and I were to receive our new badges as Waffen-Officers. But due to the bombings of the night before, there was no ceremony, just a handshake from the Obersturmführer, a new patch to sew onto our uniforms, and new hats with the Totenkopf (skull) insignia.

Figure7. Hans Bosse

There was a difference between the Waffen-SS and the German army.

Prior to 1940, it was not possible to enter the leadership cadre of the Waffen-SS with only a diploma from a secondary school. This policy changed by the end of 1940, because the Waffen-SS desperately needed new officers for its combat units. Now, secondary graduates were accepted. Therefore, noncommissioned officers changed the style of the Waffen-SS into more practical methods of leadership.

The front line of the Waffen-SS suffered heavy losses during the winter of 1941–1942, and during the Soviet counteroffensive. A few days of intensive training and I was on my way back to France again.

Mali seemed pleased to see me; my promotion must have raised my worth a little in her eyes. She opened a bottle of French wine to celebrate and the evening was very pleasant. However, I wondered if she was up to something. I hated the feeling of not trusting her, but so much had gone wrong between us.

Figure 8. U.S. Invasion of France

The bombings over Metz became more and more frequent and intense. Destruction was everywhere and people feared for their lives more and more. Mali and the children had to move out of the apartment to go live with her aunt in the country, an area a little safer than the city.

I moved out of the apartment myself and back on base.

A couple of days later, we received news from the High Command that we were to leave the base camp of Metz very soon and move closer to the German border. We all knew too well what this meant. American troops were marching on toward Metz, German troops were retreating, although this was not what we were told up front. It did not matter anymore to High Command who was qualified or not to fight at the front, and my head injuries had little meaning at this point to the Reich. Hitler was calling every man and woman to fight. Our job was to fight American troops and stop them from marching into Germany.

I was given a motorbike with a sidecar to join my division, which was now stationed in the little town of Thionville, fifty kilometers outside of the city limits of Metz. On the way there, I met up with infantry troops, and was told American troops had broken through and were not far from the outskirts of Metz. A cold sweat ran down my neck; I could not let my wife and children fall into American hands. Without a second thought, I roared my engine up and took off toward the village of Hagondange where my family was staying.

Left and right on the roadsides were comrades with machine guns, tanks, Panzer Grenadier divisions and heavy equipment, ready to stop the Americans. Some areas were impassable due to traffic, machinery and heavy blinding rain. I had to get off the main road and cross fields thick with mud. I got stuck a couple of times and didn't think my motorcycle would make it. Sliding and losing control at times, I made it finally to Hagondange.

Without even knocking at the door, I stormed in. They were sitting around the table eating dinner and looked at me as if I were a ghost. I went straight to Mali, told her to get the children ready, pack a few things and come with me immediately. Their lives were at stake, there was not a minute to waste.

Her parents interfered right away. "Mali, you and the children are staying here. The Americans are coming to liberate us and save us from those German monsters, the Americans are our allies." To my surprise, Mali left the table and gathered the children. "I am going with my husband," she said.

She quickly packed a few things, hugged her parents, and followed me outside. I placed her and the baby behind me on the motorbike and instructed her to hang on to me, and to lower herself as much as possible behind my back. I put Annita in the sidecar, covered her with my coat and secured her with the luggage, gave her a hug and told her to hold on tight. She never said a word or cried. My God, what was I thinking? We could all get killed!

Again, I raced at 120 kilometers per hour over streets and fields, my heart pounding as closer and closer came the sound of machine guns.

We were stopped at the first German post and were told Metz was now surrounded by American troops. However, they had not entered the city limits yet. The best thing for us was to get away from Metz and make our way over the border into Germany.

We arrived in Saarbrücken, a German city across the border between France and Germany. There I was told I could not go any further, and to get my family to the train station where a civilian train would leave in an hour, direction Munich. We raced to the station and everything went very quickly from that point on. I handed my family over to the railroad personnel and did not even have time to say goodbye, there was no time to waste. The transport train loaded with soldiers, civilians, and machinery was heading to Munich. There, Mali and the children would be taken to a welcome camp and be safe until plans could be made to ship them further to Frankfurt/Oder, Berlin or other directions.

16
NO WAY OUT

I returned to base camp, relieved to know that my family would be safe away from Metz. Now, duty was calling and left me little time to think. As I arrived, I was immediately told that my company was to board the next train, direction Nuremberg. I only had forty-five minutes to be on that train. This news did not displease me; from Nuremberg it would be easier for me to arrange my family's transport from Munich to Frankfurt/Oder.

After four days of riding the train, with constant air raids and many stops, we arrived in Nuremberg and reported to our new command. We had a couple of days before getting new transfer orders.

No time was lost contacting the Commando Center in Munich for news of my family. To my astonishment, I was told that no family by the name of Bosse had arrived or been on the train from Saarbrücken. How could that be? There had to be a mistake! I myself had handed them over to a Commando Sergeant and saw them board the train. "No!" I was told. "No arrivals by that name, sorry, Sir."

To make a long story short, my wife had decided at the last minute to get off the train and return to Metz with the children. I also heard that German troops were still in control of the borders, and the Americans had still not entered the city of Metz. It was somewhat reassuring.

What in the world was she thinking of, putting the children and herself in jeopardy? Being married to a German meant she could end up in jail, and who knows where the children would be placed. I was at the end of my rope.

I did everything in my power to go back to Saarbrücken and found a way to trade places with a soldier leaving for that direction the next day. I think he must have thought I was crazy. We were pulling out and here I wanted to return, but he was more than happy to exchange places. And crazy I must have been—what did I think I could accomplish once I arrived there?

I was back on the long trip over the border to France once more. The train was carrying a few soldiers returning to the French border to gather heavy equipment, arms, and material to be loaded onto return trains to Nuremberg. As soon as I arrived, I followed orders, but I needed an extra twenty-four hours to go to Metz and find my wife. I came up with an insane idea.

I told the officer on duty I had not gotten the final commando signature to let the transports out of Saarbrücken, but I was sure we would be ready by the next morning. There seemed to be no questions asked. I was breathing a little easier; it paid to be a Waffen-Officer.

I told one of my assistants I had an emergency, and if I had not returned in twenty-four hours he was to give the signed orders to the duty officer to move the transport onward and report me as missing.

Without any further reinforcement in men or material, the Waffen-SS divisions were hard put to stop the Allied advance; we had no choice but to retreat. I was delaying this mission and could be court-martialed, but I took the chance.

Two hours later I arrived by motorcycle in Metz. The streets were empty and in complete blackout. It was a mess everywhere—demolished buildings, blocked streets, abandoned vehicles, and homes burned to the ground. I knew I could do better on foot. I left my bike at the station and ran to Sablon to see if Mali was at her parents' apartment. No one answered the doorbell, the house was in complete darkness. I hoped she might be at the apartment we had rented in the city, and ran there as fast as I could through the cluttered, dark streets. I arrived, out of breath, and ran up the stairs. The door was locked; I had to knock several times before Mali opened it. She was covered in a towel and looked at me in shock. My eyes could not believe what I saw.

There, standing half-naked, was a man. I had no clue if he was French, German or anything else, and could not have cared less. I completely lost control as I grabbed my wife, hitting and hitting her until strong arms encircled me. The man, whoever he was, held me tight, telling me he had no idea she was married, and begged me to stop hitting her. I did, all strength had gone out of me. I buckled into a chair and covered my face with my hands. I never touched the guy, who at one point must have left the apartment without me noticing.

Mali's lips were bleeding, and she looked at me with contempt and hatred. I told her it did not matter anymore if she came with me or not, I was taking the children. Annita was standing in a corner of the kitchen, eyes wide with fear, and, for the first time in a very long time, ran to me crying. I grabbed Elvira from her crib and covered her with the first thing I laid my hands on, a tablecloth, I think. Mali was bent over the kitchen sink, washing her face. She said, "Fine, I'll come with you, but as soon as this war is over I am asking for a divorce." For the first time, I did not give a damn. I did not even feel sorry at the sight of her bleeding face.

We left the apartment, found my bike and headed back to Saarbrücken, arriving there at the first light of day. Again, things had changed in just a few hours. Material, food supplies, cars, motorcycles and guns had already been loaded on the train, but now they were being shipped to Posen in Western Poland instead of Nuremberg. Again, there was little time to think or plan. I had to get my wife and children on this train loaded with material and munitions. I found a wagon loaded with machine guns and helped them get in there; there was very little room to move around. Mali offered no resistance and did not speak as she climbed in. I placed the children with her and told her I would be back as soon as I could with food and water. My duties were at the head of the train with other armed soldiers watching for air raids, possible blockage on the rails, and partisan attacks.

Off we went to Posen, a trip of nine hundred kilometers. It was a slow trip. My concerns were for the children—would they make the long trip? A trip that could take three or four days if everything went well, and it was winter. I had to get food to them—and if at all possible, blankets and water—without being noticed.

On the second day of the trip, we found out we were to detour through Frankfurt/Oder. The Red Army was holding the lines and preventing the SS Panzer Corps from making the expected breakthrough. This was a miracle in disguise—I would be able to contact my parents and have them pick up Mali and the children. Also, this would be the first time they would see Elvira.

I gave the news to Mali and I was not surprised at her reaction; she refused to live with my parents and wanted her own place right away. There was no time for arguments, I made it very clear she had no choice and she would have to take it one day at a time. It was totally out of my hands anyway.

When we arrived in Frankfurt/Oder, I immediately contacted my parents from the train station and explained the situation. An hour later, Mother and Father arrived. The greetings were rather cold and Mali would not speak a word to me or to them. Mother and Father were delighted with the children and it helped ease the tension.

The loudspeakers at the station informed us that the Russians were just a short distance from entering Poland. My parents and I looked at each other without a word; it was a silent understanding. We knew all too well there was no way out.

I was able to spend twenty-four hours with my parents and family. Mali finally gave in and tried to be pleasant; my mother was rejoicing to have her grandchildren. My father and I spent half the night talking and making plans. Poland was out of the question. They would have to leave the very next morning for Leipmeriz, Czechoslovakia, with Mali and the children. The situation there was still relatively safe for the moment. The Russians were but a few days from Frankfurt/Oder and all Germans were in danger. We knew it was over and I was happy to see my father agree with me. I looked at him carefully for the first time in a long time. He had aged so much. His face was deeply lined and his hair was gray and thinning. How could but a few short years make such a difference? He looked sad and defeated; he was not the father I remembered.

17
REPRIEVE

On my own initiative, the next day I boarded the train heading to Leipmeriz, Czechoslovakia, with my family. I knew another unit of my regiment was stationed there. I could try to join them and hoped no questions would be asked as to where I came from and where I was to be stationed. I figured chaos was everywhere and this would be in my favor. I could not take my family to Posen; there was little we could do there but get all of us killed. We didn't stand a chance facing the Russians.

I showed my papers to the sergeant on duty at the train station and told him I was on special orders from my commando. Without problems, we boarded the train. Of course, I knew this could have serious consequences, but I needed to get my family out of Germany.

My parents had resources and family in the town of Leipmeriz, we just needed to get there.

However, I had no clue as to what awaited me once I reached my alternative sector in Leipmeriz.

We arrived late in the evening. I rented a horse wagon and drove through the countryside to my uncle Ulrich's farm. On the way, we were attacked by Czechoslovakian peasants. They were not dangerous; all they really wanted was food and they represented no physical danger to us. I gave them what little we had on hand and we were able to continue our route.

We reached the farm just as night fell and were warmly greeted by my uncle and aunt. I had not seen them in several years and they too had aged considerably. I had time for a quick cup of coffee before leaving and promised to be in touch as soon as I possibly could. If I could, I thought to myself.

I reported to the Commando Office and was asked to take a seat and wait. Before I realized what was happening, two armed guards came in, grabbed me roughly and dragged me to a cell.

I knew exactly what it was all about; I was in deep trouble. A day passed before I was brought in front of a military tribunal and told I would be court-martialed for desertion.

My orders had been to leave Frankfurt three days ago to join my commando unit in Poland, and here I was in Czechoslovakia. Therefore, I was considered a deserter. I wanted to tell them that the war was lost anyway and all I wanted to do was to secure the life of my family. Of course, that would not have helped in any way. Worse yet, I was taking family members out of Germany. I was placed into a cell with five other men who were in the same situation as I, deserters.

A week later, the six of us appeared in front of the military court-martial, and in less than an hour our sentence was pronounced. Execution by shooting in seventy-two hours.

I cannot even begin to explain what went on inside of me. Fear mixed with hatred was all I could feel. Hatred for this government, hatred for Hitler, hatred for the system and fear of dying were all mixed together.

This was now the end of the year 1944. I had survived a fractured skull, severe head wounds, and terrible weather in Russia; I had seen comrades die in front of my eyes, faced death many times, been broken mentally and physically, married, become a father, but had always kept some sort of hope for times to come. This was different now. The end had come for me and this was reality, there was no hope left. In the days and hours that followed, I reminisced on the course of my screwed-up life, what a mess I made of it. How would my parents, wife, and children survive?

What would be the outcome for them?

As I am writing this, so many years later, I still cannot imagine how I survived it all mentally and physically and made it this far.

The day before the execution, the six of us were called again in front of the military tribunal. We had no idea what for and could not believe the news. Hitler needed every able-bodied man at the front lines to push the Russians back. Our sentence was changed from execution to being sent to the front lines. It was for us just another form of death. We knew it was over; the Russians could not be defeated at this point. They were already on the outskirts of Frankfurt/Oder. All I could think and hope was that my parents, wife and children were safe in Czechoslovakia—at least I prayed for it to be so. There was no way to contact them and I would probably never see any of them again.

Off to Pomerania we went, toward the city of Pasewalk. I really did not care anymore—what difference was there between standing with my back to a wall to be shot down, or being shot while fighting? We were doomed one way or the other; nothing mattered any longer at this point.

When we arrived in Pasewalk it was clear what was expected of us. We were to be transferred the next morning to Zwickau and there assigned to a section called the Death Commando. We were told that in the early morning we were to report outside the barracks, line up and march on toward the approaching Russians. It was a sure death sentence; none of us would get out of this one alive. That night, lying on my bunk, it was clear to me what I would do. I was condemned to death for desertion, so what did I have to lose by becoming a real deserter?

As we assembled in the courtyard the next day, I asked for permission to use the latrines. There was one soldier coming out as I went in. I saw a window above the washbasin. I climbed onto the ledge and saw it faced the train station. I hoped no one would come in. It was not a very large window, and I squeezed through it with difficulty, jumped out and looked around, my heart beating furiously. The coast was clear behind the wagon trains. I ran to the other side of the rails where a train was ready to leave and hoped no dogs were going to bark at me and give me away.

Although shaking, I approached one of the soldiers on the platform as his dog growled at me. I acted as confidently as I could and asked if everything was loaded and ready to go. His answer was what I needed. "Yes! Herr Hauptmann, everything's ready for Leipzig." Leipzig, I thought, how much better could that be, was luck really on my side? Would I survive all this?

Leipzig is one of the largest cities in Saxony. Once there, I could plan the next chapter. Right now I needed to get on this train as fast as possible before I was found missing.

I stood in the corridor at the window, pretending to look at the landscape.

The moment the train arrived in Leipzig, air raids were going on. Wave after wave of American planes were bombing the city. It took less than an hour for a large portion of the city to be destroyed and burned.

I reported to the Station Commando and told them that due to the bombings my orders had not arrived yet. Could I speak to someone and find out what my duties were? The Commando Officer briefly looked at my ID papers, then at me. "Where are they sending you?" I took a deep inner breath and answered as calmly as possible. "Salzburg," Of course, Salzburg, Austria, was in the opposite direction from where I started. I had the proper identification papers and was in my Waffen uniform, which gave me some measure of safety. The officer turned his chair around to reach a filing cabinet. I noticed several signature stamps and ink pads on the desk and without hesitation grabbed the closest one to me.

He turned around, stamped my papers and told me to go to the waiting room to join another soldier waiting for the next departure train to Salzburg. He then waved me out without a second glance as I saluted. I almost reached the door when he called me back. My heart stopped for a moment. God, did he know I took the stamper?

"The name of the soldier traveling with you is Jakob Maile." I saluted again and with shaking knees walked out and ran to the latrines, where I locked myself in, sick to my stomach. I felt like throwing up as sweat ran down my neck; I needed a few moments to collect myself. I washed my hands and face with cold water and felt a little better. With my hands shaking, I took the stamper out of my pocket and brought it to my lips. This would come in very handy indeed; I could stamp my own papers from here on out.

The waiting room was mostly empty. I noticed a soldier sitting on a bench, dozing off. I walked up to him and asked if he was Soldier Maile? He stood up, saluted and nervously said he was. I sat next to him and told him we would be traveling together. He did not reply or look at me, just stared straight ahead.

As we waited for the train, I asked him where he was from, as he did not look to be German. He hesitantly told me he was Ukrainian-born and had enlisted in the German army. I observed him. He seemed to be a decent young man, and for some reason, I liked him. As he started to feel more confident, he told me about having lost his mother and father. An older brother had been sent east to Russia and Jakob was without news of him, probably killed. "I am alone, and have no clue what will happen next, not much chance of me surviving all this. I am trying to join some family in Czechoslovakia, if I can make it," he said sadly. "The war is lost and we'll all get killed or imprisoned anyway." I knew too well how right he was and decided that if I was to trust anyone at this late stage, it might as well be this young man.

On the trip out, we heard that the Führer had given orders for all train stations to be on lockout. Soldiers were to be assembled, controlled, and assigned back to Germany. The battle for Berlin was underway. French troops were advancing after a long detour to avoid Soviet advance columns, and of course, there were the Americans advancing as well. The only exemption for the time being was military personnel with special stamped visas.

I thought of the stamper in my pocket and looked at Jakob. How much could I trust him? I asked for his papers and told him to keep his mouth shut no matter what, our lives depended on it. He looked at me, surprised, and handed me his papers without hesitation. I stamped them and winked at him. "Just follow my orders, and all will go well." He was confused, but looked at me again and smiled.

A few hours later, we arrived in Salzburg, Austria. The station was in chaos; pushing and shouting people and barking dogs were all around. Jakob and I looked at each other, and we both had the same thought. Would our papers be valid, would it work? If anything went wrong, we would be shot on the spot.

We were very nervous as we descended the steps of the train. I thought my knees would give out any minute. I adjusted my hat and saluted one of the guards. There were six control officers and we were to wait in line.

As our turn came, Jakob in one line, me in another, I handed one of the officers my papers.

I remained ice cold, as much in control as I could, and hoped Jakob would not give himself away. I did not dare to glance at him. The officer had my papers in hand; now it was all up to him. He looked at me and back at the papers, then asked me to step aside and wait as he went inside a small makeshift office. I locked my shaking hands behind my back and looked at the other line Jakob was in. I saw he had passed the control and stood with his back turned. He slightly turned his head and I motioned him to move on.

My God, the minutes seemed like hours—what was going on? Finally, the officer returned. "Please step to the left exit." What did that mean? All others were going to the right.

I soon found out as another officer came up and said, "Everything is in order, you can move on." He returned my papers and passbook, saluted me and turned away.

Jakob was waiting a little distance away. We boarded the train separately for Dresden. Once inside, we looked at each other and started laughing uncontrollably. "We made it," said Jakob, "but who are you?"

18
ESCAPE

Dresden is a town in the state of Saxony, Germany. There, we found a little hotel/restaurant, and for the first time in a very long time, I was able to relax somewhat. I felt as if I had come back from the dead. We ordered dinner and went through several bottles of beer, got to know each other better, and I must say that we returned to the room we shared, blitzed.

The next day, we toured the town. I had to plan the next step. Jakob had become totally dependent on me. I felt that since I got him this far, I needed to include him in my plans. He was no more than nineteen years old, and at twenty-four I felt almost like a father figure to him.

We stayed a couple more days in Dresden. I grew a small beard, and bought some dark sunglasses in case someone would recognize me and a pair of slacks and a sweater.

My plans now were put into action. I changed my order papers to go back to Leipmeriz and asked Jakob if he was sure he wanted to go with me and not go on his own. He looked at me with puppy eyes. "That's where I still have some family left," he said. I knew he would follow me to the end of the world at this point. I told him it would be an extremely dangerous undertaking and I could not promise our lives would be safe. His trust in me gave me the extra courage I needed.

In Leipmeriz I would be able to see my family and children again. They had no clue what had happened to me, or I to them. I wondered if they thought I was still alive.

We boarded the train the next day and shared our compartment with other German military officers. Our first stop was the city of Aussig. I was glad no one asked questions; the mood was somber for all and with good reason. The war was lost.

New problems were in store for us as we arrived at the Aussig station. Military police came up to the train and entered every wagon. All uniformed military personnel were to get off and line up on the platform. Damn it! There it goes again, I thought. What now?

After about a thirty-minute wait, a senior officer explained that all military personnel were to be assembled and transported to the base camp at Aussig. When we arrived at our destination, our military papers were controlled. Some soldiers were sent to the right and others to the left. Jakob and I were in the right lane due to the fact that we had special passes (our counterfeit passes, of course).

We were sent to a building and told to go to office number 14 on the first floor. We passed the front building sentry, told him we were expected at office number 14. He looked at us and said, "Good luck." What did that mean? As we arrived at the front door of office 14, I had a strange feeling and whispered to Jakob to follow me and do exactly the same thing I would do.

Further down the hall was a door indicating latrines. I guess I must be attracted to latrines. We marched to it, opened the door, and as loud as possible I said, "Heil Hitler," as it was the custom when entering the office of a high-ranking commander. Jakob did the same and we closed the door behind us, loud enough to be heard from the sentry down below. Inside we waited for a while; no noise came from the hallway. After about five minutes, I slowly opened the door, looked left and right and motioned Jakob to follow me. Again we said in a loud voice, "Heil Hitler." Closed the door and marched down the stairs. The sentry looked at us in a strange manner and said, "They let you go?" We saluted him and started marching off when he said again, "You are lucky, everyone who comes out of that office is immediately sent to the front."

"Yes Sir," I said. "We have special orders for a different mission, much more dangerous."

We marched on as naturally as we could in order not to raise any suspicion. As soon as we were out of sight, we walked as fast as possible to the center of the town.

"What now?" asked Jakob. "Will we be able to get on the next train?" I looked at him. "Make sense, boy! In a few minutes they will contact the Commando Office of the station and they will start looking for us. We have to leave the town on foot."

It was late afternoon as we started walking toward the countryside. We saw a farmer with a milk wagon and asked where he was going; he had to be in Leipmeriz before nightfall to deliver milk. I shoved a few Reichsmarks Marks into his hands, and he agreed to take us to the outskirts of the town, no questions asked. We arrived just as the sun was setting. The farmer dropped us off and told us we had about ten kilometers to go on foot.

We reached town, found a café, and asked for directions to the village where I knew my family was staying. It was pitch dark as we arrived at my aunt and uncle's farmhouse.

My parents were speechless when they saw me. Mother put coffee on and prepared something for us to eat right away. I thought Mali and the children were already asleep, since there was no sign of them. Father told me she had left a few days ago to return to Metz, although the American forces were now occupying her city. She thought she would be safer there with the children rather than in Czechoslovakia where she had no one to turn to, and there was the fear of the Russians advancing.

Father said he thought it was for the best, and that he and Mother had also decided to go back to Frankfurt/Oder, despite the Russian invasion there. At least they would be on home ground with people they knew. I told him I had deserted, and to my astonishment he sadly shook his head without a word and looked away.

Two days later I took them to the train station, destination Prague. Once there, it would take a couple more days of travel to reach Frankfurt/Oder. As we said goodbye at the train station, Father put an envelope in my hands and told me to wait until later to open it. We hugged, and I had the feeling that I may never see him or Mother again. Mother was not even crying; it was as if she had lost the will to live. She put her arms around me and said: "Hansi, whatever life brings, never forget I love you with all my heart. I am so proud of you, son. It's all in God's hands now." The goodbyes were difficult—we did not know when, where, or if we would see each other again. I left them with a last hug and turned away without another word or glance, my eyes full of tears. It was to be many years before I was to see them again.

Later that evening, I opened the envelope. Father had given me enough money to get by for a while, this would help tremendously. In the following days, I was able to make contact with my in-laws in France.

I was told Mali and the children had been stopped in the town of Budweis, Czechoslovakia, and were lodged in a collective camp for displaced families. Again, this was not good news, I did not know what to do at this point, my head was spinning.

Jakob had reunited with relatives in Leipmeriz, and I was invited to stay with them for as long as I needed. The family was grateful I had saved Jakob and brought him back alive. I asked for only a few days to make plans regarding my family and rest a little. It was nice not to be on the run anymore, to have a feeling of family life and safety for a while. I could only go out at night for fear of being recognized; I had grown a beard again, and always wore a hat and the civilian clothes Jakob's family had provided me with.

19
CITIZEN OF METZ

It was now January 1945, and Germany was as good as lost. My wife was held in a camp with my two children; all I knew was that I had to get to Budweis, get them out of there and get back to France before things would get worse for them. I bid my goodbyes to Jakob and his family and promised to keep in touch, although I knew chances were very slim that I would see Jakob again.

Figure9. German prisoners in the streets of Metz.

I had shaved and wore my SS uniform. My civilian clothes were hidden in the bottom of my pack; they may come in handy again. I was lucky to get to Budweis without a hitch and set out immediately to find my family. There were several camps, and it took a couple of days to locate the one Mali was in. Again, I had to plan the next step very carefully.

After changing back into civilian clothes, I entered the camp. It was full of people speaking different languages, a dreary-looking camp with people wandering aimlessly. It took a while to get directed to a main office, where a nurse greeted me. I asked about Marceline Meyer-Bosse and her two children; she directed me to camp number 12, lagger 8 where people from Alsace-Lorraine were housed. There must have been about a hundred people in one large room with only two windows; it smelled of sweat, dirt and urine. Children were screaming and some adults arguing.

It took some time to finally spot Mali sitting at a long table eating dinner. She had Elvira on her lap, and when she saw me, she looked at me as if I were a ghost. Annita ran into my arms, calling me, " Bappy, Bappy." I sat next to them, there was no joyful reunion. I told her I would do all I could to get them out of the camp, but she had to go along with my story.

The next morning I went to see the camp director, told him my wife and children had visited relatives living in Leipmeriz while I was in Metz. I explained I was French and had lost my identification papers, but was in the process of getting replacements.

It took a couple of weeks before Mali and the children were released to go back to France. I had to wait at the camp for ID papers for myself and could not leave without proof of identification. Mali had promised to do her utmost to get civilian papers for me as soon as she was back in Metz. During those two weeks together at the camp, we had time to talk and sort things out somewhat. We realized, or thought, there were still feelings between us.

She asked if I would stay in France when the war ended. I told her I needed to sort things out first and really did not see the faintest possibility of staying in France as a German after the war.

There would not be much choice for me anyway. I could not return to Germany as an SS deserter. My parents were in the Russian district, where I could be jailed, tortured, or killed.

The Americans would imprison or kill me for sure, and God only knew what the French would do to me. What a continuous mess it was.

Mali had said her father had contacts at the police department in Metz and she was sure he would help to get French ID papers. After all, I had freed him from a concentration camp in Poland a couple of years ago when he was caught as an informer—that's another story. He owed me a favor, certainly. It all seemed to go in the right direction for now.

While I waited for news of Mali, I tried to get in touch with my parents, but to no avail. I hoped they made it to Frankfurt/Oder. What had happened to them? I reached out to Uncle Ulrich, my father's brother; he also was nowhere to be found. Were they all in Russian hands?

My papers finally arrived a few weeks later. An identification card with my photo on it. I left the camp early one morning in May with a new identity. Jean Bosse, citizen of Metz, Lorraine, France.

The trip back to Metz in a transport wagon was gruesome. Germany had fallen. Everywhere, ruins upon ruins, smoldering homes and buildings, dead cattle and horses in the fields, the smell of doom everywhere. Abandoned tanks and machinery for miles and miles, people pushing carts loaded with the little belongings they had, and children sitting on top. The rain was pouring down and some carts loaded with furniture were stuck in the mud. Fear and exhaustion were carved in everyone's faces.

We crossed into France and within an hour, the train pulled into the Metz station. Before I stepped off the train, I saw two civilian-clothed policemen checking everyone out. I did not know if this was good or bad. Mali was nowhere in sight and I had a fearful premonition. The moment I stepped out of the train, the two policemen came up to me. "Are you Hans Bosse?" I was bewildered, was I Hans or Jean? My German accent left no doubts about who I was. Without waiting for an answer, they handcuffed me. What was that all about?

I was taken to the Metz Police Department. The inspector was relatively friendly, perhaps because I was married to a French woman and had deserted from the German army?

I was given two choices, being incarcerated as a political prisoner or going to a camp for prisoners of war. I knew too well the difference between the two. A political prisoner had little chance of survival and could be shot anytime. Whereas a prisoner of war would be sent to hard labor camps in most cases, and at least, with a little luck, would survive. I chose the prisoner-of-war camps; it still held some hope, I thought.

Mali had been behind all this and had been paid to get me arrested.

20
WAR PRISONER

The war was lost and the Fatherland lay crumbled. Hitler had committed suicide in Berlin on April 30, 1945, with his lover Eva Braun.

The coward had ended his life, unable to face the consequences of his crimes. And we, thousands and thousands of prisoners, were now being punished at the hands of our enemies.

I was taken by truck to a prisoner-of-war camp and found myself among thousands of men from all over Europe. The conditions at the prison camp were terrible. We were cramped by the dozen in a small cell, in bunk beds above bunk beds with straw mattresses, dirty blankets, and lice driving us crazy and causing sores that became infected. Mice and sometimes an unfortunate rat or two ran along the baseboards; many times they served as a meal to some. There was very little food besides a watery soup given once a day, stale black bread, and sometimes a chunk of potato or some type of root, if we were lucky.

I was lucky enough to have a lower bunk bed in a corner; it allowed some privacy. I had found a loose plank under the bunk bed where I hid my writings, which I did late at night by candlelight. Writing was my mental escape.

Weeks went by, it was now early July 1945. There were over ten thousand war prisoners in our camp alone. Every day we saw guards carrying three or four bodies out of the camp; some had died of hunger or disease, some committed suicide. We could hear the French guards laughing and saying, "Another Kraut out of the way." We were treated like animals, called all sorts of names; they spit on us, and the ones not swift enough at work were beaten. Deep down, could I really blame them? How many thousands and thousands had we killed? If we had won the war and had French prisoners in our country, would we have treated them any different? We took turns clearing the minefields and each night some bunk beds remained empty—we knew why.

With the little food we were given, I had lost weight and was skin and bones; sometimes I thought it might have been better to have been shot. But I held out, and was surprised not to have health issues as in the past. Still, I had no news from my parents, my wife and children. We were totally cut off from the outside world. The same question went over and over in my head. Why did Mali do this awful thing? Had we not planned to have a new start after the war? Had she not provided French identification papers for me? What had gone wrong?

One morning, we were told to assemble outside and were divided into small groups. I had befriended another German soldier in my cell and we both wondered what this was all about. I told him we needed to do all we could and stay together.

It was announced over the loudspeaker that every able-bodied man was to be sent to different locations for labor. If some of us had the necessary qualifications for a specific job, we were to step out of the line and let the guards know. The loudspeaker screamed Masons, Mechanics, Carpenters, Electricians, etc. My friend looked at me. "What are we waiting for?"

As I was going to answer him, we heard, "FARMHANDS." Immediately I thought food, and told him to raise his arm. We both stepped to the side, along with a dozen other men.

We were led outside the walls of the camp and saw eight farmers with wagons and horses. My buddy looked at me. "Are you crazy? I have never been on a farm in my life." I told him I never had either, besides being around horses. We needed food and working on a farm was the best way to get some; it did not matter what the job was.

A dirty-looking farmer came up. He looked us over, felt our arm muscles, shook his head and told us to climb onto his wagon. The guards had him sign papers and off we went.

His name was Mr. Archen, from the village of Budange, about fifty kilometers from the city of Metz.

Oh! The smell of freedom, the green landscape, fields of wheat and poppies all around; it was the most beautiful sight I had seen in a long, long time. I inhaled the fresh air so loudly that the farmer turned around and gave me a mean look. "If you guys try anything funny I will shoot you on the spot." And for good measure he put his shotgun on his lap.

When we arrived in Budange, my friend and I were separated. He was to go to another farm in the village of Fameck, a few kilometers further. I almost laughed when I saw the look of panic in his eyes. I winked at him, he winked back and sighed. I whispered, "It beats the cell and the hunger we have known, we survived and now we can learn how to work the land."

We arrived at Mr. Archen's farm, a small white building with chickens and geese running loose everywhere, a barn with cows, and a small enclosure with three pigs. The smell of manure reminded me of the horse stalls of my youth at my father's. He introduced me to his wife, Mrs. Marie Archen, and asked me to follow him upstairs, where he showed me my room. A real bedroom to myself! A real bed? I could not believe my eyes; there was even a window looking out over the land. Was this real or a dream? In a gruff voice he told me dinner would be served at seven sharp, then turned and left me standing there speechless. There was a washbasin in my room and I scrubbed my face and hands for what seemed forever. The smell of soap and the feel of water was a delight and a luxury almost forgotten.

Dinner was out of this world, I had to restrain myself from gulping the food down and tried to be at my best. The three of us ate in silence.

I was dismissed soon after to my room, and told to be ready for work by 5:00 a.m. the next day. Again, he emphasized that if I tried to escape there was little chance for me, I would be caught in no time and shot. If I did my job as asked, there would be no problems.

As soon as my head hit the pillow, I fell into a deep untroubled sleep for the first time in a very long time.

21
BETRAYAL

The next morning, my new life started. I woke up to the most delicious smell of coffee and went down to the kitchen. I was told to help myself to coffee, bread and jam. Would the wonders ever cease? Was this a dream from which I would soon wake?

Mr. Archen showed me the property. In the barn were eight milking cows, looking at me suspiciously. I was told to milk the cows every morning at five, and in the evening again. The next small building housed four horses, which I was to brush daily. I was also to clean the barns, get rid of manure, bring in fresh hay, clean the chicken coop, gather eggs, and feed the pigs.

I would have no problems with the horses, cleaning manure and bringing in fresh hay, but COWS?? I had never touched a cow in my life, least of all milked one.

Mr. Archen looked at me in a strange way as he asked, "Are you a farmer, Bosse?" He smirked and added, "I think if you are a farmer, I am General Charles de Gaulle. I give you two days to prove yourself or I will take you back to camp, is that understood?"

I could tell he had no sympathy for me, there was even hatred and contempt in his eyes. I had to learn fast; there was no way I would go back to the prison camp.

It was a small property, beautifully located at the edge of a forest where one could disappear, I thought. But to what good? Where would I go? I would be quickly caught to face a worse fate. At least here I had a good job and food, even if I was hated.

When he left the barn, I turned to the cows. I could tell by the way they looked at me that they did not like me either. They must have sensed I was German. I placed the milking stool behind the first cow as I had seen it done in magazines. However, she slapped her tail back and forth and hit me in the face so hard I fell off the milking stool. I heard someone laughing. Mrs. Archen had been watching me. I was red with embarrassment as she came up and pushed me aside, not paying attention to my excuses. "Here, young man, let me show you before my husband sends you back."

Two days later, at dinner, I was told that I could stay on. I had realized from the first day that Mrs. Archen wore the pants in the house. She smiled and winked at me as if it was a joke between her and me.

Sometimes I wondered what my father would say seeing his son milk cows and scraping manure. It might have brought a smile to his face. The thought of it warmed my heart.

The days went by. I started putting on a little weight and feeling human and happy again, even felt like singing at times. I also was given some decent clothes to work in.

After the first week, Mr. Archen seemed pleased. Though I would only see him at dinnertime and he hardly spoke or gave me the time of day. Mrs. Archen sometimes invited me to have a cup of coffee with her; I think she was lonely and needed someone to talk to. I felt comfortable and started confiding in her. She was a kind woman who reminded me a lot of my mother. I told her about my family in Germany, my wife and children in Metz. She was astounded, and told me if I wanted her to, she would inquire about my wife the next time she had business in Metz, which would be the following week. I gave her the address of my in-laws and thanked her profusely.

The day she went to town, I was nervous the entire time until she returned late that evening.

I found her alone in the kitchen before dinner. She told me she would get with me as soon as she could and not to mention anything in front of her husband. In his eyes, I was nothing but a German prisoner, and he couldn't care less about my personal life.

I had to wait until the next afternoon, when Mr. Archen was in the fields, to speak to Mrs. Archen. I was on pins and needles. She told me she found my wife at the address I had given her, and had been able to speak with her. Mali was doing well, and had given birth to a healthy little boy on July 11 of this year; his name was Jean-Pierre. What? I was the father of three children now?

Three or four months passed and it was now February 1946. Mrs. Archen came to me one day and told me that she needed help driving the horse wagon to Metz to sell chicken and eggs at the Saturday morning farmers' market. It had snowed heavily the day before and the roads were in bad shape.

I was happy to have a little distraction from the daily monotony. There was no work in the fields now and I hoped I would be kept on to do the odd jobs. My daily fear was to be sent back to the camp.

I knew there was no chance to see Mali and the children while in Metz. I was a prisoner and would not get very far before being arrested should I choose to run away. I would not want to get Mrs. Archen in trouble by any means, she had been too good to me.

We arrived at the marketplace. Suddenly, in front of me stood Mali with Annita, Elvira and a baby in her arms. I was speechless. Mrs. Archen had arranged all of this. She gave me a few francs, told me to go to the café across the street and to be back to return to Budange with her at two in the afternoon. She warned me not to do anything stupid, my life depended on it.

I spent two hours with my wife and children. I held Elvira in my arms; she was very curious and kept staring at me. She was now almost two years old. Annita seemed very reserved toward me, and there was this little seven-month-old baby. Mali asked if I wanted to hold him and placed him in my arms.

I scanned his face intensely. He had narrow blue eyes, blondish fuzzy hair and no resemblance with his sisters, who both had red hair. There was the strangest feeling as I held this baby—what if he wasn't mine? I tried to reason with myself. What gave me this insane thought? Mali told me it had been a very difficult birth. She had almost lost him; he was born early, at the seventh month, she said. I looked at him, calculating in my mind, then looked at her again and saw such sincerity in her eyes. I was ready to believe anything. Still, that strange feeling would not leave me.

We talked and talked over our cups of coffee, now cold. I asked her if she had anything to do with my arrest. She looked surprised, and said that when she had not heard from me after several days, she went to the police department, where they informed her of my arrest but would not tell her where I had been incarcerated.

I told her I had a good life at the farm I worked at, and hoped I would be released soon. With the war over, I wanted to try to return to Germany with her if she wanted. She did not reply, just looked away. I also knew it was a dream for me to think of going back to my homeland.

When we parted, we promised each other to write regularly. Perhaps Mrs. Archen would need me to drive her to Metz someday again, I told her.

On the way back to the farm, I noticed that Mrs. Archen was deeply lost in thought and seemed troubled. Little did I know that again, a surprise was in store for me.

During dinner that night, Mr. Archen told me for the first time that he had a son, Albert, who was released from the military and would be home in a month's time. "Therefore," he explained, "my son will be back on the farm and I will no longer need help. It has been arranged for you to return to the military prison camp in Metz." I was speechless, it felt as if someone had hit me in the chest. I left the table to return to my room, sat on the bed with my head in my hands.

Dear God! I cannot go back to that prison, be hungry again and mistreated. I would rather die.

In the days to come, I asked Mr. Archen if there was any chance I could see my friend Helmut once more, the one who came with me and was working in the next village. He agreed and I was able to see Helmut for a short time. He looked great, had put on some weight, and looked much stronger. He said he was happy enough with the family he worked for, but wanted to get back to his own family in Germany. I told him that I was to go back to the prison camp in Metz, and he was stunned. I explained that I had an idea, and if it worked, we could both go back to Germany in three weeks' time. He was in full agreement, but wondered how. I just told him to sit tight, not to say a word to anyone, and wait until I knew more.

I asked permission for my wife to come and visit me at the farm. It was granted; Mr. Archen seemed a little friendlier toward me these days. Probably because he knew I would be leaving soon. I wrote Mali and asked her if she could come and see me as soon as possible, it was urgent.

She arrived three days later. I told her I was to be sent back to the camp and that I would do all I could to avoid returning there. I needed false ID papers for two people. I explained I had a comrade in the next village, and our plan was to cross the border and return to Germany for a short time. As soon as I was safely there, I would send for her and the children and we could start a new life. I begged her to help me; French police were watching all train stations carefully, and some German prisoners had recently tried to escape and been shot on sight. The French government was paying 1,500 francs per prisoner to anyone denouncing Germans.

I also asked her to provide me with sulfuric acid, which she could get at a pharmacy. She looked at me puzzled, put her arms around me and said she would do everything she could to help. She only asked that if I sent for her and the children to come to Germany, she would not go to Berlin, but would stay closer to the French border, where she could still visit her family regularly. I agreed and made her that promise.

A package arrived from her a week later. In it were baked goods, a letter and a bottle of sulfuric acid. She wrote that she would be in possession of the papers in a few days. It was too risky to mail them, so she would let me know the day she could come and meet me at the village.

I had to get rid of the tattoo under my arm, the tattoo that would give me away as an SS officer.

I applied the acid to it as well as on the other side of my arm to make it look like a gunshot had gone through my arm. The burning was terrible, I wanted to scream. It was the only way to get rid of the tattooed ID and not be identified. My chances would be much greater as a simple enlisted soldier.

I was to meet Mali at the Budange village train station the following Sunday morning. She would be there with the children. It would look more like a family reunion, she said, and would attract less attention from the French police.

Over the months, Mrs. Archen had given me a little allowance for paper and pen when I needed some; she knew I loved to write. I saved and had enough money to secure two train tickets to Metz for Helmut and me; all we needed were French IDs for the both of us.

Once in Metz we would take a train to Saarbrücken, Germany, and from there it would be easy for us to disappear, each in our own direction. Mali assured me she would have everything ready in time.

I needed to get together with Helmut and work the time and day out. It was easier than I thought. Mr. Archen had to visit someone in Helmut's village to take some bales of hay there and could use my help. He agreed to let me meet Helmut one last time to say goodbye. Helmut and I met for a few minutes on the main village square later that afternoon. As we sat on a bench, I told him of my plan and we decided to meet on the country road before daylight the following Sunday morning. From there, it would be easy to get to the station on foot, where my wife would meet us. "Wear your cleanest clothes," I told him, " and also a head covering, like a beret." We needed to look like French farmers.

It all went as planned. I hated not being able to say goodbye to Mrs. Archen and deceiving her, but I had to do what I had to. Helmut and I met and arrived at the station at daybreak the following Sunday. There were only a few people and no one paid attention to a couple of farmers. Two policemen stood guard on the platform; the train had not arrived yet. The sight of the two men made us very nervous, but we acted as normal as possible.

I saw Mali with Annita and Elvira; she did not bring the baby. I went to her and hugged her tight. We acted as if we were family; Helmut carried Elvira in his arms and I had Annita by the hand. I gave Mali the money and she went to the cashier to buy our tickets. A few minutes later she returned, handed us the tickets and our ID papers. She said she would take a bus back to Metz with the children in order not to raise any suspicions; the bus would leave in thirty minutes and she would be waiting for us at the Metz train station when we arrived. I really did not question her, but wondered why she thought it would look suspicious to travel together. However, I was too nervous to give it much thought. She would be waiting for our arrival at the Metz train station and would have the next tickets for us to board the train for Saarbrücken, Germany. She kissed me, shook Helmut's hand, grabbed the children and rushed out.

As we arrived at the Metz station ready and excited to get off the train, Helmut put his hand on my arm and pulled me aside. "Something is not right, Hans. See these three policemen?" I looked over at them. They were checking everyone coming off the train. "Do you think they are after us?" I said. Helmut's shaking hand took mine and said, "Hans, just in case, thanks for everything, but I am not returning to the prison camp. Good luck to you." I grabbed him but he pulled away and started running toward the other end of the train, where he jumped out on the rails side. All I heard were gunshots as someone grabbed me roughly by the shoulders, pinned my arms behind me and handcuffed me.

"You dirty Kraut," said one of the policemen, "your friend is done with and you are next."

I couldn't see Helmut anywhere, it must have been him who got shot. I was dragged off the train, and then, my eyes could not believe what they saw. Mali was standing next to two French civilian-clothed policemen; she never looked at me. I was thrown into a car and driven to the police department in Metz. What was happening? What had happened to Helmut? Did Mali have anything to do with this?

At the police station, I was taken to a small windowless room and pushed into a chair. I was alone for what seemed to be a long time. All I could think of was that Helmut had been killed by my own fault, and I was going back to the lagger prison camp.

It had all been planned so carefully by Mali—what had gone wrong? Did Mr. Archen guess something and turn me in? Had Mali turned me in? She had told me that people were paid to turn in any Germans trying to flee.

The door opened, someone came in and took off my handcuffs. It was a tall man, fat and bald, who looked at me with hatred and a dirty smirk on his face.

"You are married to Marceline Rose Meyer, yes?" I could only nod. He was writing something on a notepad. "And you are Waffen-SS Officer Hans Bosse?" Again I nodded yes. He walked to the door, opened it and turned around.

"Bosse, I will share something with you. You were denounced by your own wife. She came to us a few days ago and we helped her with the paperwork. In exchange for her loyal services, she received 3,000 francs for two German war prisoners." He started laughing. "You filthy Krauts, you really thought you would win this war?" He laughed out loud and slammed the door behind him. I sat there, dumbfounded. How could she have done this horrible thing? One man was dead because of her, and she got 1,500 francs for him. I just sat there, too numb to think or feel anything. My hands were shaking uncontrollably.

The next day, I was transported back to the lagger and put into a dark cell. Water and bread was all I received for ten days. It is difficult to believe that a human being can survive on bread and water alone, but I did. I kept my sanity by thinking of the farm, the cows, the horses and Mrs. Archen's kindness and delicious meals. Thank God I had been fed well on the farm, or I would never have survived those ten days.

22
A FREE GERMAN IN FRANCE

One morning, they took me out of the cell to join other prisoners. My eyes were burning from the daylight; I thought I would go blind. There were about four thousand of us left in that camp. The prisoners looked miserable, skinny, sick, half-clothed and with little will to live. We were all assigned to hard labor and mine removals. There was no pencil and paper this time, no corner bunk bed for a little privacy—the conditions had worsened since I had left. The smell of unwashed bodies and the stench of excrement were unbearable at times. It was no longer the French who took the dead bodies out to be buried, it was us. I have to admit there were times I wished I was one of those bodies. I knew in my mind I would not last much longer; the will to survive had left me along with Mali's betrayal and Helmut's death. I wondered how the German prisoners fared under the Americans. I had heard that they were just as hateful and brutal as the Germans had been.

Several weeks went by doing backbreaking work, de-mining and splitting and stacking rocks from morning to night—rocks used to rebuild the much-destroyed city of Metz. The most fearful times were spent out in the fields to dig up mines and disconnect them. My hands were most unsteady, and each time, I thought it would be my last moment.

I befriended someone from the eastern region of Germany. He was a farmer by trade. His farm was now in possession of the Russians and he had no news of his wife and children. I told him what I had learned at the farm in Budange, and how well I had been treated. His name was Herman Schultz. He had heard rumors that once a month, the French were looking for farm or land help and that we should try to get out of here; we still looked strong enough. I was all for it, but why would they let me go again? The only chance on my side was that I was relatively fit and in good health so far, whereas so many prisoners were sick and weak, and no one wanted them for outside jobs. Could luck possibly be on my side again, just once more? I prayed for one more chance in this lifetime.

And luck it was—a farmer by the name of Josef Muller needed three prisoners to work the land on his farm for two months. He picked Herman and me, but no one else was fit for the job. All he said was that we would have to do the job of three men, with no pay, just food and board, and that he would have an eye on us all the time. I thanked my lucky stars for a couple of months' reprieve and food again. How long were we to remain prisoners? How long would I last?

The farm had sixteen horses, forty-two hogs, eighteen milk cows, and numerous sheep. He was probably one of the wealthiest farmers in the region. The work was hard from daybreak to dusk, and we would fall in bed exhausted at the end of the day. But we had food, plenty of fresh air, sunshine and most of all, I was a pro at milking cows now.

From my wife, there was no news. I could have cared less at this point, I was done. I wanted nothing to do with her again and knew I would never see my children again either. They would grow up fatherless, or another man would raise them in time, but even that thought brought no emotions on my part. I had given up, really given up this time. There was no future for me, no hope for a better life, no hope to see my parents again. I knew I would die eventually in this foreign country I hated.

One day, a letter from my parents arrived; it had taken six months to get to me. I could not believe that the letter had passed through, and my eyes blurred as I read.

Father wrote that they were so happy to have found out I was alive; he did not say how he had found out. They only knew I was in a prison camp in France, location unknown, and had sent the letter to the German city hall in Berlin in the hope it would perhaps get to me. For them, however, things had not turned out so well.

The family home had been taken over by Russians and they were now under Russia's regime. They had been given a small apartment to share with another family and were on food coupons. Food was hard to come by and they lived frugally on the little they had. Most of the time, they had to hide what food they had from the other family sharing the apartment. Everyone was starving. Father had lost his job at the courthouse and was working in a factory, assembling wires and sorting metal for Russia's armies. Their health was all right, and Father found solace in books, any books he could put his hands on. Uncle Ulrich and his wife were on the west side of Berlin; they had lucked out. But Father could not have any contact with them. Mother did not write but sent her love through Father; I wondered how she really was. They were not telling me all of it, I guessed that much.

It was unbelievable for me to think of Father working in a factory under those conditions. I had never seen this proud man but in a suit and tie. And now my parents were under the Russian regime, facing hunger and the unknown. Here I was, their son, eating plenty at the farm and unable to do anything for them. The cocky boy I once was, the one who wanted to join Hitler's Youth against his father's wishes, was regretting it so dearly now. If one could only undo the past and make things right... Would I ever see them again? I knew Father was not a physical man. I feared for his health, and how was Mother handling it? Would the nightmare ever end? I wondered why I came into this world.

Summer turned into fall, two months had gone by, and I expected Herman and I to be sent back to camp before the winter. We thought of running away but knew it would never work. Where would we go? To our surprise, we were told that we would be needed for a longer period of time. We were beyond joy. And before we knew it, it was spring 1947. I had been a prisoner of war for about two years now; it had become a way of life for me.

One day, my employer came back from Metz with news from the French Ministry. Every German prisoner of war had the possibility for freedom, if for two years he would work for minimum wage at whatever job he was assigned by the government. After that time, he would be free to leave France. Mr. Muller, my boss, explained what was really going on.

The French government no longer wanted German prisoners on their hands. It was a way to get rid of us, but at the same time use us for whatever labor they had in mind for a time, at very little cost to them. But some of us would not go back to Germany after two years were over. Political prisoners like me would be sentenced to death or hard labor in my own country. I had thought mistakenly that with the war over I would be able to return home. The others, nonpolitical prisoners, would be welcomed back as German fighters for the Fatherland, and probably hailed as heroes by some. However, Herman was very happy with this deal. He had been a simple soldier who had been taken prisoner. He would go home in a couple of years, look for his family and go on with life the best he could. For me, it was another story—I could not go back as a political prisoner, I had no home to go back to, and I did not want to fall under the Russian regime. Also, I had three children, whether I wanted to or not, whether they knew me or not. What choice did I have but to stay in France? Oh God! What is ahead? The thought of committing suicide was often on my mind, and to this day I don't know why I did not go through with it.

I filled out the necessary papers, and two weeks later I was a free German in France—a limited freedom though. I received a visa from the police department, and was told to report every morning at the police station. Mr. Muller did everything possible to keep Herman and me as his laborers at the farm. He was not the one paying our wages—the government would pay us weekly, and it was to his benefit to have free help. But he had turned out to be a decent man and treated us well.

Being free meant that I could leave the farm on either Saturday or Sunday after receiving my meager pay. I could go where I wanted within the limits of the village and stop at the café for a beer, although former prisoners like me were not welcomed by the locals. They merely tolerated us and called us names. But, as time went on, they became used to our presence and we were somewhat better accepted. Sometimes we even played cards or billiards with the French men, who in this area of France spoke mainly German.

Once or twice in the first six months, I took a train or bus to Metz with permission of the authorities, but had to be back before nightfall. Metz was being rebuilt. It was a huge undertaking; the city had been incredibly destroyed. The reconstruction was unbelievable—all the historic monuments were being worked on to look as they once did, but it would take many years to complete such a huge project.

I never went near my wife's family home, although I longed to see my children again.

Life went on at the farm as usual until the day came when I took leave of Mr. Muller. Two years had gone by, and I was now a real free German man, free to make choices and decisions. No more reporting to the police, and I was able to look for a better-paying job. Herman went back to Germany and I moved to Metz. I envied him being able to go back to his country with a family waiting for him and find his roots again. Your heart always remains where you were born, I realized sadly, and I longed for my homeland.

However, there were no jobs to be found. Everywhere, doors were slammed in my face.

With the little cash I had on hand, I found lodging in a warehouse where other displaced and homeless people lived. It was only a step away from the prison life. The stench, the dirty straw cots placed next to each other that gave very little comfort or privacy—does one ever get used to those conditions? This was not for me, I had to find work no matter what. I didn't care what it was as long as I could afford a single room, and have a little food and privacy.

The money ran out fast and still I had no job. I was now really desperate and on the verge of begging in the streets. I went to the courthouse to ask for an extension with the promise to repay as soon as a job opened up. I was given a few hundred francs and told that a percentage would be added to repay the loan. Three days later, I saw an advertisement in the paper for workers needed as pitmen for the coal mines. I applied, no questions were asked and I got the job. I had learned to milk cows, I could learn to be a miner too.

The hours were long—eighteen hours per shift, six days a week. I needed the job desperately; it meant food, lodging and a more normal life. The mines were located in Falkenberg, about sixty kilometers outside of Metz. I had free lodging ten kilometers from the mines in the village of Morange where other miners were lodged. A bus took us back and forth daily.

I had absolutely no knowledge of mining, and looking back on it today I can only say it was a miserable frightful job.

I wore the only clothes I owned, not much to speak of. My first paycheck went to buy work clothes and shoes, and to repay my loan. The lodgings were no luxury, but I had a room to myself, a bed, sink, table, stove, chipped dishes. Heat only at certain times of the day.

Every day at 3:00 a.m. the bus picked us up. Worn-out men shivering in the cold morning air, faces lined with grime that soap was unable to remove. No one spoke, we all just sat there exhausted, dozing during the trip to the mines. When we arrived, we were given a mining lamp that fit around our heads, dirty overcoats and boots. Up to six men would jump into a cart on rails that would take us down into the bowels of the earth. The darkness, the claustrophobic feeling, the sounds down in the mines are unexplainable and unbelievable for someone who has never been there. You could hear rumbling sounds of the earth, coal dust falling, loud cracking sounds. I never knew that the bowel of the earth was so alive. Each day going down, none of us was sure to see daylight again and come out alive. Many of the men had families and had done this job for several years. Most were old beyond their ages, some were coughing endlessly and spitting up black phlegm. This was all they knew to make a living and survive. One has to have worked in the mines to know the daily nightmare it was, the courage it took to go down daily.

It was dark from the time I got up at two thirty in the morning, and by the time we would resurface, around eight thirty in the evening, it was dark again. Sundays were the only time I got to see the sky, a sky mostly gray and rainy, which is the norm in the province of Lorraine. But I was so tired, I slept most of the time anyway.

23
DIVORCE

One day, there was a collapse in another area of the mine. About sixty men never made it out. However, work went on as usual, as if nothing had happened. No one spoke about it and I realized that these brave men were used to it. They never knew if or when their time could come, if they would see their families at the end of the shift. I befriended no one; there was no time for chatting or creating friendships, just breaking up the coal for hours, loading the wagons one after another, on and on and on.

Twelve months passed until the day I decided I could no longer continue. Inhaling coal dust every day was causing breathing problems again. I had coughing spells that would last longer and longer, and I would spit up a black substance, then the asthma attacks started again. I was going insane in all this daily darkness and finally gave notice; again no questions were asked.

I pocketed my paycheck, cleaned up my room, and took the next bus to Metz. The one benefit of the job had been the pay. I had saved practically twelve months' worth. I had needed very little for myself during that time, and now had enough to live comfortably for a few months without worries.

I found a small apartment on the outskirts of Metz in a quiet neighborhood. An elderly widow was renting a room and bath in her house. She made it clear, no women, no parties or drinking. She had nothing to worry about, it was the furthest thing from my mind at that time. I slept for three days solid, had the luxury of a bathtub and spent a lot of my time soaking and soaking to get the grime off.

My skin took forever to get clean, and the taste of coal was constantly in my mouth. I coughed up black phlegm for many months.

Eventually, I started feeling better again and decided to confront my wife one last time.

I wanted a divorce now. I bought a used suit, shirt and shoes and set out to my in-laws' house.

Father Meyer opened the door and, after realizing who was standing in front of him, hugged me. "My God, Uli, you look terrible! Where have you been?" He explained they had thought I was dead with no news of me for such a long time. "Mali never heard from you after she visited you at the farm," he said. "We knew a lot of prisoners went back to Germany, some were deported for political trial, killed or locked up." I realized then that he knew nothing about what took place at the train station, the killing of Helmut, and my arrest. I decided not to say anything about it and asked about Mali and the children. He told me she lived with two of the children in an apartment in Metz; Annita was still here with them. Elvira and Jean-Pierre lived with Mali and she worked as a waitress at some bistro in town. I asked to see Annita. Father Meyer told me she was not home, she was with her grandmother in town. He gave me Mali's address. I was grateful for his kindness toward me and longed to tell him what had happened, but did nothing.

I knew, had his wife been home, she would have slammed the door in my face. I thanked him and left.

I found the bistro where Mali worked, entered and ordered a beer, looked around but did not see her. When I asked, the owner told me it was her day off.

I set off to the address of her apartment. It was not very difficult to find and was located in a secluded area of Metz, rather middle class, with a garden and flowers in the front.

It was a two-story apartment and her name, Marceline Meyer, was printed next to the second-floor doorbell. So, she was Meyer, not Bosse. Was she able to pay for this apartment with the hard-earned money she received as an informer to the French police, or did she have a new lover? Probably both.

I rang the doorbell but no one answered. I decided to wait and didn't care if it took hours; my anger was boiling again. Across the way was a small park where I sat on a bench, determined to wait.

It wasn't too long before I saw her walk up the street, pushing a pram. A little four-year-old was tagging along—Elvira, I thought. I could not see the child in the pram. Mali looked very well, her long black hair tied in the back, smartly dressed in high heels.

I crossed the street. "Hello, Mali" was all I could say with a lump in my throat, hating any emotions I still felt. She turned her head, saw me, and after a brief moment of surprise her eyes turned cold and changed to hatred.

"What do you want?"

I told her we had to talk. "I am going to see a lawyer and file for divorce. I want rights to see my children."

She started laughing. "As a German, you have no rights to your children or to anything else in that matter."

I looked straight into her eyes and said, "They are my children, regardless of if we Germans lost the war. If you decide to act in a friendly manner it will be a lot easier. Here is where you can find me." I wrote my address on a piece of paper, handed it to her, turned and walked away. My heart felt as if it would break—how could I ever have loved this woman?

I was given the name of a lawyer by my landlady. Mr. Wagner was his name. Little did I know that this man, in the years to come, would become a friend and mentor to me. When I met him, he was very reluctant to help me. I had little money, and of course, I had been an enemy of his country and not very welcomed. I told him my story and could see interest building. He scratched his head, looked straight into my eyes and told me to give him a couple of days to think this matter over. I left thinking he would probably not take my case; money would be the biggest issue.

A few days later, I received a note in the mail. Mali asked me to meet her at a café in town the following weekend. When I arrived, I realized it was the same café we had gone to when we first met, and returned to many times afterward. It seemed a lifetime ago. I wondered if she was up to a trick again by asking me here.

I arrived first and took an isolated table near a window. She came in a few minutes later. I have to admit, she was a beauty and so easy to fall for. However, there was no way she would ever get under my skin again, I swore to myself.

She sat down, smiled amicably and ordered a café crème, then her look changed to contempt as she said,

"We do need to talk! I want a divorce as well and have started procedures, the law is on my side and you can understand why." Yes, I understood why, I stood little chance to have any rights to my children; they were French and I was an enemy of the country.

I told her there would be no problems with a divorce, she could have it. However, I wanted rights to see my children and I would cause no problems. She looked at me with sudden interest and I could see she was thinking.

"Well! I have a lot of problems with Elvira," she said. "She is a difficult child, always has been hard to handle and very unruly. I am looking at placing her full time in a Catholic institution. As far as Jean-Pierre is concerned, he is moving in with a foster family in two weeks' time. I do have a difficult time making ends meet with two children."

"Yes," I said, remaining calm. "I can understand, what about Annita?"

"Annita is happy with my parents, they have raised her since birth, and will keep her. So, I am all for this divorce. I need child support and a normal life with you out of it."

I looked at her sadly. "Mali, you don't care for the children. It is clear they are actually in your way. How can you split them up like this? They have a right to know each other and grow up together." She just looked away as I paid for our drinks.

"It's your call," she said. And left the café without a second glance.

I made an immediate appointment with Mr. Wagner, my lawyer, who received me kindly but with a little annoyance in his voice.

"I asked you to give me a little time to think things over, Mr. Bosse." I sat down, sighing heavily, and told him about the meeting with my wife.

He seemed pensive and said, "It would probably be easier if both parties agreed on visiting rights with the children, and you paid child support." He then gave me the good news that he agreed to represent me—if somewhat reluctantly, I sensed.

Two weeks later, I received a letter from my lawyer advising me to talk things over with my wife; he had sent her a similar letter. If we could come to an amicable agreement, it would be less expensive that way.

He would be willing to meet both of us and draw up the divorce papers.

I met with Mali again and after a long debate we did come to an agreement, which I knew was to her benefit. She could not care less about raising the children, all she wanted was her freedom. After arguing back and forth, it was agreed that I would take Elvira to live with me. Mali would give up all rights to Elvira if I signed an agreement to raise her, and she was never to come for help of any kind, or to see the child again. I would pay child support for the other two children. It was hard for me to believe how easy it was for her to give up Elvira.

As for Annita, I knew that her grandparents would fight to keep her and I promised to never interfere with her upbringing in any way. Regarding Jean-Pierre, I had a question. "Is he mine?"

She laughed. "Of course he is, any doubts? You will have Elvira, Annita stays with my parents, Jean-Pierre is in caring hands and that is the end of it. You can accept or not, we can meet the lawyer and talk about our agreement. Then, get out of my life once for all and you will never hear from me again either."

A couple of weeks later, the papers were signed and the divorce was in progress. My lawyer told me that Jean-Pierre had been placed in an orphanage. Mali could not afford for the time being to have him with a foster family. Annita was to remain with the Meyers, and I had Elvira.

What a mess, I thought, three children who would never get to know each other, never grow up together. I left Mr. Wagner's office with a terrible weight inside of me. I still had no idea how I was going to raise Elvira, I didn't even know the child.

I found out where Jean-Pierre was placed and visited him. A nun dressed in white took me to a small metal-framed bed. My heart broke for him, he was so little and frail, and just lay there sucking his two middle fingers and looking up at me. He was in a long narrow room with about thirty other little metal-framed beds. I picked him up, hugged him and placed him back in his little bed with the strange feeling he was not mine. I left the orphanage with a heavy heart.

I went to visit him a couple months later and found out he was now with a foster family. I would not see him again for many years.

I searched for a suitable apartment; my present landlady wanted no children on the premises. I eventually found a furnished apartment a little larger and sunnier than the one I had. It would take a bigger chunk out of my income, plus I would be paying child support. But I had no choice if I stayed in France. Then, I set out to find work. Mali had agreed to give me the time needed until I found a decent-paying job.

I found a masonry job in Metz; those jobs were easy to come by with the city undergoing major rebuilding. The pay was decent, not great, but would cover my immediate expenses.

Through my landlady, I found a woman who did childcare in her house and would take in Elvira during my working hours. Things were somehow working out, for better or worse. Mali brought Elvira to me one Sunday morning. She handed me the child's meager belongings and a couple of toys. I emphasized again that she was never to come near Elvira again; she shrugged her shoulders, hugged the child and left. Was I imagining tears in her eyes?

24
IRMA

Elvira was now a little over four years old and mine to raise. I had never been around children and felt at a loss. Dear God, was I crazy?

A new life had begun for me. Every morning I got Elvira fed and dressed, took her over to the sitter, and went off to a job I hated. Picked her up again around six in the evening, fixed dinner, gave her a bath and put her to bed. This was the daily ritual, and I sensed the child was not happy.

Mali had been right; she was a difficult child, and very stubborn. The sitter had the same problems with her and I feared she might not want to keep her. I have to admit that the only way to make her obey was a few good spankings, which she came to respect in time, but there was little bonding between her and me. She seemed to resent me the moment she laid eyes on me, and I started regretting my decision more and more.

At work, I met a young Hungarian man by the name of Etschi, a foreigner like me. We became friends and in time he helped me find someone to stay with Elvira on weekend nights when we went out. I was young, free, and eager to have some long-overdue fun.

Etschi and I loved dancing and we became regulars at a dance hall in Metz. He had a girlfriend who took me aside one evening. She had noticed that I was often picking fights with other men and always leaving the dance hall with a different woman. "Don't you want to settle down?" she asked. I told her I had no interest in a permanent relationship, I was a divorced man raising a child, and I let her know I was a little upset at her interference.

She was very persistent though, and told me she had a girlfriend who was a war widow from the country of Luxembourg. She lived in Metz, also had a child, and spoke perfect German and French. I figured I had nothing to lose and agreed to meet this woman the following weekend.

Figure 10.   Hans, 1948

I came earlier that Saturday night and stayed at the bar drinking a beer, waiting for my friends to arrive and to see this woman before we were introduced. It was not very long before they arrived, accompanied by a cute blond girl. I liked her looks. They came up to me and introduced her as Irma. The band started playing a tango and I invited her to dance. She was easy to talk to, spoke fluent German, which helped a lot, and danced to perfection. We didn't speak about our private lives, just enjoyed dancing together all evening and made a date for the following Saturday.

I went back to my apartment that night feeling a little happier and less lonely for the first time in years.

We met for a couple of weekends before I asked her out to dinner. That evening we confided in each other. She had a little boy, Daniel, seven years old. Her husband had been a French fighter pilot and had been shot down when she was a few weeks pregnant. She lived with her sister and mother in Metz, and had not returned to her country of Luxembourg when the war had ended. I told her about my life, my parents, my ex-wife, my three children and the custody of Elvira. This was the first time I was able to talk to someone about it and I felt such a relief to be able to talk about my life. She seemed

Figure11.   Elvira, Daniel, and Hans, 1948

to understand and did not question anything, just offered her support. We met a few more times, and before we knew it, we spent many Sundays together, taking walks in the parks with the children, confiding in each other.

I found out she had taken part in the Resistance, had been caught and sentenced to prison for a few months before the war ended. A friend of hers in the South of France had taken care of Daniel during that time. After her release, she could not find work at first and take care of her child. She left him with her friend for a total of four years. When she came to get him back, the child wanted nothing to do with Irma, and still had a difficult time being away from the woman who raised him and whom he thought of as his mother. Daniel and Elvira were getting along very well. Daniel was three years older than Elvira and seemed to be protective of her. It was nice to have this distraction in my life, a sense of normalcy again.

However, things did not go over very well with Irma's family. Her mother and sister were against her seeing a German, a good-for-nothing, as they called me. She stood firm, however, and we decided to find an apartment together and share our expenses. She was a seamstress and could work from home, which would save on childcare for both of us.

This was now Christmas 1948, and we were poor but happy. I felt a new life starting for me; Irma was a strong and stable woman and I loved her more each day. In time, her mother and sister accepted our relationship and a kind of truce came between us. But like with the Meyer family, my ex-in-laws, I never felt totally comfortable but did not ask for more.

My divorce was final in early 1949, and Mali was out of my life for good. She kept her word and never tried to contact me or see Elvira.

Through friends of Irma, I found a new job as a mechanic with a large company; this increased my income considerably.

During that time, I also obtained a French driver's license and started looking for driver jobs. I soon found one and was hired as a truck driver/delivery man during the week. I left my mechanic job and found another job on weekends driving excursion buses and translating from French to German or vice versa. My command of the French language had greatly improved with Irma's help, even if my accent gave me away.

I tried to see Annita a few times to no avail. At her first communion in May 1949, I went to the church where it took place and stood at the back, just content to lay eyes on her.

Of course, no one knew I was there and I left the service before the end. Sometimes, when time permitted, I would go near her school, park my truck and see her come out. She was now a little over eight years old, had not seen me in a long time, and would not recognize me. She had long dark auburn curls, seemed very serious for her age, and always walked out of the school alone, not like the other kids who were with friends and played around.

Would I ever get to know her in the years to come? I wondered often what had happened to Jean-Pierre. I had gone back again to the orphanage, but he was no longer there and they refused to tell me where he was.

From my parents, there was news once in a while, and what news there was always made me upset, worried and sad. The letters were censored and they could never write freely about their lives; sometimes pages were missing. I tried to read between the lines and could tell they were most unhappy and in financial need. There was no getting them out of East Berlin, and there was no way for me to go in to see them either. I sent care packages to the address I had, but most of them never got delivered, I later found out. The Russians appropriated most everything. Nights for me were the worst, that was when the thoughts would go rampant in my mind and peace was hard to find. How could I get them out of East Berlin?

25
MEETING ANNITA

In October 1950, Irma and I were married. It was a small wedding with only her mother, her sister and my friend Etschi, who was best man. We had found a larger apartment that felt luxurious to us and celebrated our wedding there. Irma had done all the cooking ahead of time with the help of her sister. It was a very happy day for both of us, but the thought of my parents made me sad.

I wished they could have been part of my happiness and met this wonderful woman. I had one more wish and it was to have a child with Irma, although we could hardly afford another mouth to feed. That wish came true, however, in January 1955, with the birth of a little girl we named Nicole. Times were very difficult for us between 1950 and 1953; money was tight.

I worked seven days a week and Irma worked late into the night sewing for clients. But we were young and the future lay ahead of us.

In 1953, luck came my way and I was hired as a salesman by a large company called SUZE, an importer and exporter of wines and liquors. The only drawback was I had to travel all week, which left Irma alone with the children. Elvira continued to be a difficult child, and Irma did her best with her upbringing. But as the years went by, Elvira came to love Irma as a mother and they had a great relationship.

After a couple of years, because I was fluent in French and German, I was promoted to commercial agent and later trained in the trade of wines and liquors. From then on, life smiled at us, and we moved again into more comfortable lodgings. I was happy with Irma and had come to love her very much; she had a way of calming my anxious and tempestuous temperament, and she was a steady and trustworthy woman. The years went by and the children grew up.

Our lives had their ups and downs, but overall it was a good life. I had gotten used to traveling and Irma got used to my absences.

On August 13, 1961, the Communist East German authorities built a wall that totally encircled East Berlin. More than three million East Germans had escaped to West Germany over the years; most were young and educated, and the Russian wanted to keep them on their side. Moscow was not pleased and decided to do something about it to stop anyone from entering or leaving. This was when the wall was erected.

It was a terrible shock to me; my parents were now totally cut off from the West, and living poorly in subsidized housing. In those days, the Western Deutsche Mark was worth four to six times as much as the Eastern Deutsche Mark, and the Cold War intensified. Those in the East realized now that there was no escape for them, and living on the edge of poverty had become the norm.

The wall was 155 kilometers in perimeter, with electric contacts, observation towers and dog runs, and it was guarded by more than eleven thousand Russian soldiers. Still, the young kept trying to escape every day at the risk of their lives, and many lives were lost, according to the news we got in the West.

I kept contacting the authorities to free my parents, to no avail. As long as one was productive and in good health, the Russians needed them. News came more and more infrequently from my parents. I knew they could not get mail out and tell me the truth about their living conditions. Therefore, the little news I received was always tinted in a rosy shade. However, I knew in my heart that things for them had to be bad, and it ate at me day and night.

It is now autumn of 1965, as I am writing this last part of my life.

Annita is a married woman living in the United States. I was happy to have made contact with her in the years before she left. She had never been allowed to see me and did not know me until she turned eighteen, and found out I lived in the same city as she. I could understand, she had no curiosity or desire to get to know a stranger. Too many years had gone by and so much had happened in her life too. I found out her younger years had not been a bed of roses.

I also found out that Mali had remarried and had taken Annita and Jean-Pierre back to live with her and her new husband. Annita was then nine years old and Jean-Pierre five. Mali had turned into an alcoholic, and for five long years, the lives of the children became a nightmare until social services finally stepped in and took them away from her. Annita was in poor health due to neglect and was sent for one year to a sanatorium in the French Alps. After recuperating, she went back to live with her grandparents, who had been granted custody. She was then fifteen.

I never saw or heard from Jean-Pierre, who had been placed in an orphanage until he turned eighteen and joined the army.

I met Annita for the first time in 1959, by chance at a dance hall in Metz. She was eighteen and it was at her coming-out ball. She was there with her aunts and uncles, and I was with Irma and friends when I spotted my ex-sisters-in-law four tables down from us. I guessed immediately who the young woman with them was.

She was a little beauty with long auburn hair, no resemblance to her mother at all.

I took my chances and went over to their table to ask permission to dance with Annita. She had absolutely no idea who I was; I only made myself known to her at the end of the dance. She looked at me in surprise but never questioned me. I remember to this day how she smiled and said, "So, you are Bappy?" I had forgotten it was the name she called me as a child and tears came to my eyes—she had remembered. I placed a folded piece of paper in her hand with my address and phone number on it, but really never expected to hear from or see her again.

I was to be wrong; she did call me and came to the house. From that day on, she visited Irma and me regularly, but never told her grandparents where she was going. We got to know each other, and I had but one regret—never having seen her grow up. I realized more and more how much she resembled me in many ways. She had a curiosity for life, a great need to learn, and a wonderful sense of humor.

I never told her about my past and never mentioned Mali to her. It was she who brought Mali up and told me about her life with her mother. It made me sick at heart to hear what she and Jean-Pierre had gone through in their young lives. The poverty and abuse they experienced was incredible. Why was I not surprised how life had turned out for Mali?

Two years later, Annita met an American soldier, married, had a little girl named Karina and left France to make her home in America. How ironic that I once tried to save her from the

Americans, and now she was going to that country to make her life there. She gave me the blessing to be godfather to Karina, her first baby. I could only wish her happiness in her new foreign country. I knew too well how hard it can be to leave one's roots, culture and homeland behind, and I hoped she would never suffer from it as I had over the years. When one leaves one's homeland and has to learn a new way of life and a new culture, one never really fits in totally, no matter how many years go by. There are always differences that set you apart, and the longing for the land of your birth never leaves you.

Elvira and Daniel are also married and have children now. It leaves Irma and me with the youngest, Nicole.

26
NOVEMBER 1, 1965

As I sit here today finishing these memoirs and looking back on all those years, from the young man of seventeen to the man of today, I must say I was not always the bravest but neither a coward. Life has not been easy on me. I did things I am not proud of, it was wartime and survival was all that mattered to any of us then. I never hurt anyone willingly, but had to do what I did at the risk of being killed myself. I live with my phantoms day and night and still have nightmares frequently. Many times an uncontrollable sadness submerges me, but there is no way to alleviate the heavy burden.

My parents still live behind the Iron Curtain. I was granted a special visa to visit them two years ago for only three days. Three beautiful days it was. I was not allowed to bring them any goods as I had wished; what I had was taken from me at the border.

This was the first time I had seen them in over twenty years. I did not recognize them at first. Father looked old and worn out for his early seventies, but he still worked at the metal factory. Mother could not stop hugging me, looking at me and hugging me again and again, crying bitterly.

We spent as much time as we could talking, but I never gave them many details of what happened during the war. Why bring on more pain? Mother never complained, never talked about the life we once had, she just looked sad and broken. To surprise me, she had baked one of my favorite childhood cakes, chocolate cake, and I know it must have meant a lot of sacrifices to get the ingredients. I had to force myself to swallow past the lump in my throat, remembering my early childhood days. How easy it had been then, how little any of us knew of what the future held in store, the pain and sorrow that was to come, the horror of it all.

The days went by too quickly and it was time again to say goodbye. Father hugged me tight when I left and said with a sad smile: "Hans, remember always, life owes us nothing. I am proud of you and always will be."

The lump in my throat was getting bigger and bigger as I slipped some money into his hand. I held him tight, not knowing when or where I would see either of them again. Mother hung on to me; I thought she was going to break down, but she did not. She smiled through her tears. "Hansi, someday we will be together again," she said. I don't think she believed in her own words, but I smiled and hugged her tighter, hating to let her go. My heart was breaking.

I walked off, looked back at them, and waved one last time. Saw the dingy gray apartment building they lived in, the empty sad-looking street, the darkness of it all. I walked away as fast as I could, tears running down my face. I felt so helpless and empty.

I am saving these writings of my life for my eldest daughter Annita in the hope she will someday understand, not judge me too harshly, and forgive where I went wrong.

I have loved her as much as I possibly could. My wish is to someday be able to give her these writings personally. If not, my hope is that they will not be destroyed and will be forwarded to her.

A bigger wish yet would be to visit her someday in her new country, hold her children in my arms, be the father and grandfather I never had the opportunity to be.

Be well, dearest daughter, may life be kind to you, may you find the happiness your childhood denied you.

Bappy forever.

PART II
ANNITA

27
WHERE DO I BEGIN?

Eighty-three years into my life, I have the same questions my father did when he wrote his memoirs so very long ago.

This is the year 2024. Many years have passed since my father wrote his story and left it to me. He came to visit me in the US in 1972. At the time, I was in the midst of moving to Colorado, and I packed the unread journal in a box along with some photos. Forty-four years later, by chance, I found the long-forgotten memoirs. Years after his passing.

I had to read them over and over several times before I could undertake the task of translating them from German into English. I went through such a mixture of emotions, feelings of denial, bitterness and anger. But Father, through the lectures in your writings I got to know you better, and little by little I was able to accept your side of the story. For so many years, I had been influenced by the French side of my family and its history. I never got to know my German side, my unknown heritage and family.

I would like for my children, grandchildren, great-grandchildren and family members to understand us a little better, and perhaps others may have an interest in our memoirs and history as well.

Through your writings, I got to know you so much better, more than I ever thought I would.

I had an image of you that did not match what I found out in later years. It was the image of a selfish human being, a murderer, as my French family called you. A sort of brainwashing had been done as I grew up, to protect me, I guess. I cannot blame them; they suffered so much at the hands of the Germans through World War I and II.

My years growing up were not easy ones. I was not only the daughter of a German man, but also the daughter of an SS soldier and a French woman. Many people of my region, Alsace and Lorraine, had fled the oncoming troops and went to safer areas of France, mostly down south, where they had families to welcome them and, in many cases, hide them. After the war, when they returned to their homes, or what was left of them, they had not been obligated to speak German as we were. My family did not have the luxury of escaping and had to live under German rule during the entire war.

The German language was mandatory and anyone heard speaking French was deported into camps. Therefore, I did not learn French until I started school at age six. However, it gave me the opportunity to speak fluently in two languages early in life.

I left France for America in 1963. Father, although you and I had met a few times before my departure, we never had a real father–daughter relationship until many years later.

Even though thousands of miles separated us, we got together each time I flew back to France, and we corresponded regularly. Over the years, you and your second wife became an important part of my life. The guidance of a father came late, but nonetheless it came.

You and I took many wonderful trips, and I discovered Germany through your eyes. To my astonishment, I felt at home in Germany as much as I did in France, and came to love your country. The language was no barrier for me, having learned it as a child. I became fond of its culture, music and people. So many years had to go by until I found you and my roots.

We even took a trip together to San Francisco once, just you and I. It was an unforgettable trip.

My French grandparents had passed away, and I no longer needed to worry about hurting their feelings because of our relationship. They never forgave you and sadly took that hatred to their graves.

Then, one day in 2001, my life collapsed. You left this world in the most tragic way by committing suicide at age eighty-one. You shot yourself. Your wife—Mama, as I called her then—had passed away two years prior. Your mental and physical health had become a concern to all of us.

I flew home immediately when I heard the news. I hated what you had done and could not accept or condone an action I called cowardliness. I had lost you again! In my selfish view at that time, I felt you had lacked the courage to go on. How could you have done this to your children and grandchildren? I felt such a sense of abandonment.

But as the years went by, I started understanding and was able to forgive. However, so many years later, it still hurts and I miss you.

I remember reading the following words somewhere, and they spoke to me.

**IT HURTS, SAYS THE HEART,
YOU WILL FORGET, SAYS TIME.**

BUT I WILL ALWAYS COME BACK... SAYS THE MEMORY.
—Author unknown

You left us a brief note, the last words of a man who had such a passion for writing.

I still have your poetry and unpublished novels. You were a writer at heart.

To my dear children,

I beg each of you from the bottom of my heart not to be angry at me and to please forgive me.

I am unable to avoid what I am prepared to do. I tried very hard to continue to live but cannot make it anymore, it has become too difficult.

I think of Mama day and night and have tried very hard to accept her absence, but can't make the sad and heavy thoughts go away. I don't know if you will understand me. Your point of view is probably very different from mine. I feel so very alone, Mama and I lived together for 52 years of a loving relationship. Not to have her anymore has become unbearable.

The days have become more and more difficult to face. I can no longer bear the emotional and physical pain I am going through. For this reason, I have decided to put an end to it all and rejoin my Irma.

Once more, I ask for your understanding and forgiveness. I may be leaving you, but I carry you in my heart. One thousand kisses to each one of you.

Your loving Father and Grandfather.

How often have I wondered what went through your mind and heart during those final days of your life. The last hours, minutes and seconds. Did it take courage to pull the trigger before the last curtain fell?

> I remember reading this quote that made me think of you.
> **Your voice has faded, but i remember it so very well.**
> **I remember how you sounded when you were happy, sad, or angry.**
> **In my memory your words live on as though it is a favorite book i read over and over. A collection of lessons learned, even if at the time i did not understand.**
> —Author unknown

A couple of weeks after your passing, I wrote you a letter. A letter to soothe my troubled mind and soul.

> *Wednesday, May 16, 2001*
>
> *Dear Father,*
>
> *It has been a while since I last wrote you. I had no idea at the time that it would be my last letter to you in this lifetime. You left in the blink of an eye.*
> *I am seated in front of my keyboard, my heart heavy with enormous sadness, and I miss you.*
> *You decided to leave and go to Mama, as you wrote in that last letter to your children.*
> *I really don't know where to start, I only know I need to communicate with you once more.*
> *Where are you? Do you hear my pain? Or is the world beyond just a great void in which we ignore everything?*
> *I remember that after Mama's passing, you could not accept that she was not giving you a sign from where she was. I told you then that she was still with you, but in another dimension. She had only left on the physical level.*

Easy to say, right? Here I am today, trying to communicate with you and looking for the slightest sign. Alas! Nothing.

However, this morning as I was looking out of my kitchen window, the little chime you had given me long ago was ringing lightly and there was not even a breeze. Then, a little bird perched on it, looked at me and flew off. Was that a sign? One can believe anything in moments of need.

Two weeks ago, on April 29, 2001, I was at our mountain home in Grand Lake, Colorado, when the phone rang. It was Elvira, my younger sister. From the tone of her voice, I guessed something was wrong. She was sobbing and all she could say was "He is gone, Annita, he is gone." Not understanding, I asked her where he went; I thought perhaps he had taken a drive somewhere. Through her sobs, she said, "He killed himself this afternoon." The blood drained from my body and I screamed into the phone that it was not possible, it could not be true, HOW . . . HOW??

But it was true, you took your life. Something you had threatened to do many times since Mama's passing, but none of us took you seriously.

I flew to France the next day with Robert, my husband.

The last time I had seen you was just before Mama died two years ago, in 1999. You disappointed me so much with your daily drinking and anger toward life. I swore to myself I would never come back home to see you again. I was angry too.

But you see, I did come back to see you once more, too late this time.

Elvira had already cleaned the apartment of all traces of blood on furniture and walls. She did not want anyone to see the mess you had left behind. How she had the courage to do this, I will never know. I looked at the apartment where I so often came to visit you and Mama these last thirty years. I looked at thirty years of memories, furniture and photos, and I could still hear the laughter of each time I was with you both. But now I could not even cry; there seemed to be no emotion in me other than anger. The same anger I guess you felt at one time.

I was told it happened around 4:30 p.m. The neighbors who looked in on you each day found you with the rifle still in your hand.

What terrible loneliness, what sorrow, what pain had been yours? A pain none of us children understood. You were prepared, since you left that final note in which you asked for our forgiveness. Your neighbors told me that the last time they drove you to the cemetery to visit Mama's grave, you kissed the tip of your fingers, put them on her photo and said, "I will come soon, Irma." They saw that you had already put your photo next to hers. Of course, they did not make to connection of what was to come.

Did it take courage to do what you did, or was it an act of cowardliness? I thought you were the most selfish person, only focused on yourself. Had my grandparents been right about you after all?

We had been a very dispersed and dysfunctional family. I was, and had been for many years, only a part of your life via long distance.

My brother Jean-Pierre suffered all his life from your coldness and indifference because you had never been sure he was your son. And, in fact, he was not.

Elvira was always there for you when you needed her, but where were you later in life when she needed you?

Daniel, Mama's son from her first marriage, always held resentment toward you because he witnessed a lot of your anger and rage.

Nicole, the daughter you had with Mama, seemed to be the only one you really loved, and the only one who escaped your wrath.

To this day, I still wonder if you loved me. I knew there was a fatherly love, but I never really felt it, not real love. I did not grow up with you and we came into each other's lives too late, I think.

When I saw you at the mortuary, I stayed alone with you for a few minutes. I looked at your face; you seemed to be peaceful and asleep. The wound at your right temple hardly showed, your right eye and cheek were bruised, your nails were blue. But besides that, you looked as if you were sleeping. I thought what a great job they had done to hide the wound.

You wore your favorite burgundy sport coat, the one I remember so well.

I put my hand over your heart and asked if you had loved me, an answer I will never have.

I murmured in your ear that I would try to forgive, thanked you for giving me life and for the good times we had too late in life.

I went to the door, turned around one last time. Told you I loved you, to be at peace, and walked out.

Little did I know then that somewhere in my belongings, forty-some years later, I would find your memoirs. Find out who you really were, and that you had loved me a lot, in your own way.

I remember one of our last phone conversations when you asked me for my bank account number. You said you had saved a little money in my name and wanted to transfer it to me.

I told you to keep it and take a vacation instead. But you insisted it was mine and that you were putting your affairs in order. You talked about perhaps coming one last time to America to see me again.

You would call almost every morning at 6:00 a.m. Those calls were heavy on me; I could not understand your daily laments, your lack of strength, the loneliness of your life. Looking back, I can only feel so very sorry. I did nothing to help you, or at least to try to understand what you were going through. We are so self-centered when young and only realize it later in life.

Now, I wake up sometimes at 6:00 a.m. and wish to hear the phone ring once more.

Last night, I called your number in the hope of hearing your voice on the recording. It kept ringing and ringing, I guess it had been disconnected. How I remember the way you would answer the phone.

"Allo! Oui!" And when we would hang up, "Goodbye, my darling." You would always send two kisses over the line. The very last time we spoke was when you were hospitalized for a mild stroke. You were weak and could not speak very well, but your last words were, as always, "Goodbye, my darling." Except that time there were no kisses at the other end.

Still, I have fond memories of us; we did have good times together. I remember our trip to San Francisco in 1983, our laughter and jokes. I cry for you, Father, and at the same time I hate what you have done through your suicide. But the day of your cremation, when I saw the heavy incineration door open to let your coffin slowly disappear inside, my sorrow was enormous. It was the end; you were leaving me forever now.

Have you found peace? Are you reunited with all those you missed so much and who have gone long before you?

You know what hurts now? My German heritage left with you; you were the last link to my past. I am now the eldest, and there is no elder left to turn to, no more family, either on the German or the French side. All the others are younger and know nothing or so very, very little about what our lives have been. Suddenly, I fear my own mortality. I fear getting old and sick, and being alone. How ironic to think that's what you went through at the end, and I did not or could not understand.

I ask myself, toward what are we going? What is the reason for our passage on this earth?

I can hear you answer me in your philosophical way. "It's life, birth and death, my darling, and we can only do the best while on this earth."

Perhaps now, Father, you have all the answers. And, who knows, someday I may find out as well. Until then . . . I love you, Bappy.

I FOUND THIS POEM SOMEWHERE.

It was you

Yesterday i closed my eyes and asked for a sign, and there you stood your eyes shinning, so clearly in my mind. I reached out to you, as the light shone on your face.
I felt your loving arms around me as you wiped my tears away. It was you,
It was you.

And just today as i was waking, i looked into the sky and there i saw
An eagle fly, all alone so high. It circled right above me, like an
Angel's gracious flight. And i heard its cries echoing around me.
"everything will be all right."
It was you coming through, soaring through.

And just tonight with darkness falling, there came a gentle rain tumbling
Down, so soft and slowly sounding out your name. Its song was like
No other, it was just a sweet refrain from long ago.
I felt your love falling around me, washing away my pain. It was you.
Somehow i knew, it was you.

-Author unknown

28
ANNITA CÉCILE WALBURGA

Don't forget—no one else sees
The world the way you do,
So no one can tell the stories
You have to tell.

—Charles de Lint

October 2023

As I look back on the road traveled, I realize no one forgets, but we have to move on.

However, it helps to look in the rearview mirror at times and see who we were, where we came from, and where we think we are going.

Going over the stages of my life has taught me that while we cannot undo the past, we can change the way we understand it and feel about it, and we can choose the meaning of our experiences.

As Robert Frost wrote, "In three words, I can sum up everything I learned about life: It goes on."

I hope to leave something behind, not only something of myself but also something of those I have loved, whose lives have touched mine and who have crossed my path on this earth. Those now long gone, from whom I inherited my culture and, in essence, who I am.

Retracing my memories over the span of so many years and recounting the roads traveled, I see some filled with doubts and fears, sadness and pain, but also many of them lined with joy and beauty.

Each road and detour has been a strength builder; the sunny and rainy days somehow seem to mingle into one as the years go by.

I remember so well . . . seeing older people as I grew up, thinking that these folks were so many years away from me. Back then, I could not imagine in my wildest dreams what it would be like to become old and broken.

Now I have reached the stage where my friends are getting old and gray. They move slower, no longer as vibrant and full of life as they once were, and some have already long gone.

As I enter this new season of my life, I find myself unprepared for the physical changes. Winter has slowly crept up, but I have no regrets, it's all part of life. It feels like I stayed younger for so long and did not see myself getting old. I do hope to continue being a participator in life rather than a spectator.

On November 13, 1941, I came into this world in the midst of World War II in the city of Metz, Sablon, in the province of Lorraine on the northeast side of France, bordering Germany.

My city was occupied by Germany. The country had declared war on Poland on September 1, 1939, and France fell to Hitler in June 1940.

I was born at the home of my maternal grandparents, Marie and Jacob Meyer, delivered by a midwife, as was common in those days. I lived with them until the age of nine. My mother was almost nineteen when she gave birth to me and was not yet married to my father, who was at the front lines. There is no need to go over their story, since it was previously told in my father's memoirs.

However, I would like to give a bit of the history of my hometown, Metz. My heritage and culture.

Lorraine, of which Metz is the capital, has beautiful rolling green hills and is best known for its production of coal, steel and white wines. Its closest neighbor is the province of Alsace, which was also occupied by Germany.

These two provinces, caught in wars between France and Germany, have changed nationalities many times since 1871.

Centuries of strife have created border citadels around the cities of Metz, Toul and Verdun, while most of Alsace, the sister province, abounds with castles built to guard strategic locations in the past. Both provinces were seized by the Germans at the end of the Franco-Prussian war in 1871 and became German territory. They reverted back to France after World War I and were seized again by Germany in 1940, to be restored once more to France at the end of World War II. Many scars remain to this day in these two beautiful provinces.

The first Germanic invasion happened in the year 275. Metz was totally destroyed and later rebuilt. During the first and second centuries, Metz was an open city without walls. In 1324, the city surrounded itself for the first time with high walls, and had eighteen entry doors.

Most of these walls still stand today. The city has a long and tormented past, which forged the character of its natives. People of Lorraine are reserved and not very demonstrative, perhaps because they always lived at the edge of danger throughout history. Germany meant fear, and constant changes in culture and language have long been the norm for people in the region.

At the northeast frontier of France, bordered by the Rhine River, lies Alsace—a fertile watershed between the Vosges Mountains and the German Black Forest. Lorraine, on the other hand, with its rolling landscape, is the poorer cousin, but it is more overtly French in character.

At the time I was born, Lorraine and Alsace were suffering again from German invasion with the outbreak of World War II. Immediately, German became the mandatory official language. Anyone heard speaking French was immediately jailed or deported to German camps. Street and shop signs were changed to German names. This is why, at my birth in 1941, I was issued a German birth certificate. This certificate also bore the swastika because my father was an SS soldier at that time. I was a child of two different cultures, French and German. I was to live with this stigma and suffer from it for many years to come.

Later in life, however, I finally was able to get a French birth certificate.

Wars do not stop human feelings and often love has no barriers, which was the case for my mother and father. They met at the worst time and under the most adverse circumstances, but love was, and remains, the universal language.

I have little memory of my father until I reached adulthood. My mother was never a significant figure in my life either, until I reached the age of nine. She and my father had three children: myself, my sister Elvira and my brother Jean-Pierre. However, Jean-Pierre was from another man, as it was found out later. The three of us did not grow up together, and we had no relationship with our parents for most of our lives.

The first four years of my life were filled with the sound of falling bombs, explosions, dead bodies in the streets, airplanes flying over our home, air raids and running to safety in the cellar in the middle of the night.

June 6, 1944, known as D-Day, must have been a glorious day for the people of France when the Allies landed. There was finally light at the end of a long tunnel.

From the beaches of Normandy, the Third American Army under the command of General Patton was moving toward Lorraine and Alsace. However, they were stopped by the German army, and it took two more months before American troops could move on again.

Metz was finally liberated on November 20, 1944.

Figure12.   1943

29
OMA & OPA

Figure13.   My Mother, me age nine months, and my Father. The Flower is an Edelweiss from my Father.

I had a loving childhood with my grandparents, but suffered a lot for being the daughter of an SS soldier. Kids did not want to play with me and called me a Kraut. At school I was made fun of, called many nasty names, and the teachers, who were Catholic nuns, made me salute Hitler and click my heels in front of the class when I was called to the blackboard.

The absence of and lack of love from a mother and father shaped my entire life.

My grandparents, Oma and Opa, as they are called in German, occupied the second story of a modest but beautiful apartment. The large kitchen windows overlooked vegetable gardens, fruit trees and, in the distance, the church steeple from which the bells rang throughout the day and night. It was the sweetest and most comforting sound throughout my growing-up years.

They rang the hours, rang for weddings, baptisms, funerals and disasters. Each function had a different sound. I was baptized in this lovely church, in the same white lace gown my mother and her sisters wore at their baptism, as was the custom in those days. Today I think of what a legacy this was.

Figure 14. Oma in her late fifties.

My Oma was the first to hold me at birth, and over the years my bond with her was the strongest I had, along with my Opa. They were the parental figures I was never to know with my own mother and father. Oma's nickname for me was Maiika. I don't know where that name came from, but perhaps she did not like the name Annita that my father had chosen.

Opa was very protective of me, and I loved him dearly. Of average height, perhaps five feet eleven, with white thinning hair, he was a very quiet man who loved his cigarettes, wine and rum. He seldom laughed, but when he did, it came from the heart and his pale blue eyes would light up.

Figure 15. Opa in his sixties.

I remember a large blue tattoo on his right arm representing an anchor, and on his left arm was a series of numbers tattooed from time spent in a labor camp. For reasons still unknown to me, he had been arrested by the Gestapo during World War II and sent to a labor camp in Poland, where he spent several months before my father was able to pull strings and get him released. There was never any talk at home that I know of. My father mentioned it once to me many years later. But he never told me why Opa had been arrested.

Opa worked long hours as Commander in Chief at our main train station of Metz. It was a big title, but with little income.

What I remember the most as a child was going to church with him. On Sundays, he was the bell ringer and would let me pull the thick ropes, which lifted me up and down as the bells chimed—it was such a thrill. Perhaps it is why, to this day, I still have a love of chiming church bells.

I always feared Oma's reactions more than Opa's; he left the discipline to her entirely. She was a very strict woman and always stood by her word. She was short and plump, with dark hair and brown eyes, not very demonstrative by nature, always with a serious look on her face. However, her love showed in everything she did and in the sacrifices she endured while raising me on a meager income. She never complained, and went about her household duties day in, day out, with none of the luxuries we enjoy today.

Laundry was done by hand in our clawfoot bathtub, then hung out to dry outdoors, or in the cellar during winter months. There, the clothes would sometimes freeze, and we had to continue drying them inside the warm oven before wearing them.

She was a superb cook and baker. Our garden provided all the necessary vegetables, which she canned for the winter months. She was, in my opinion, an intelligent woman who never had the opportunity to learn, but she had curiosity about everything. Her main outings were for grocery shopping and church on Sundays. When I was a little older, she would often ask me to teach her French. I cannot imagine what her life must have been. Women in those days did not question their lot in life.

In order to save electrical power, the lights in the house were never turned on until dark or until the lamplighter came at dusk in the winter months. He was an older man, and long before you could see him coming up the street, you could hear his voice.

"All is well, dear folks, have a good night."

He carried a long gaslit stick with which he would light the street gas lamps that stayed on for three hours each evening. Only then would Oma close the shutters, turn on the electric lights in the kitchen and start the evening meal. How sweet were the days of the lamplighter and how comforting a way to end the day.

I would often sit on Oma's lap while she told stories. One I never forgot was about gnomes cleaning the forest during the night and everything being clean and bright the next morning. My child's mind would envision all these little people being busy while I slept.

There were times I would sit on Opa's lap, hold his hands in mine, and question all the brown spots on them. "They are earth spots," he would say, "and when my hands turn all brown, I will return to earth." I did not understand the meaning and would constantly check his hands, waiting for them to turn brown.

I have very few memories of my maternal great-grandparents. However, I do remember Oma's brother, my uncle Ernest. He lived in Paris and was a language professor. I loved his visits once a year; he was always dressed smartly with a hat and cane. It was he who offered me my first dictionary at age fourteen. I still have it to this day, now worn and faded. He encouraged me to always be curious about life, to study and become someone I could be proud of.

Oma had married my Opa, Jacob Meyer, early in life, at age sixteen. She had practically no education but was always of a curious nature and loved reading. In those days, her reading mainly consisted of the newspapers. I had heard she quit school at age fourteen, entered into the service of a family as a maid and there met her future husband, my Opa. She came from a small village in Lorraine by the name of Liederchidt. She always missed her home and family, but was rarely able to return to her place of birth after her marriage. Although the village was only three hours away by train, people rarely traveled in those days. For all their lives, Opa and Oma depended on buses and trains. A car was unheard of.

Each year in the summer, we would spend a month's vacation at a beautiful mountain chalet my grandparents rented with other members of the family. It was called Chalet Aurore and had beautiful views over forests and valleys. I still have such fond memories of times spent there running through the woods, picking berries, and going to the little village of Budange for milk and eggs with Opa.

Dinner was always my favorite time—all of us around a big wooden table conversing, laughing and sharing the day's events.

Sadly, I don't remember much of my mother during those years, although I am sure she must have been present at times. I figured she had to work and did not have much time or desire to be a mother. I did not miss her; I was happy with Oma and Opa.

30
MEMORIES

I vaguely remember bits and pieces of trips to Germany, Czechoslovakia, Yugoslavia and Poland during the war with my father and mother. Such faded memories. I was too young to remember until I read my father's memoirs. Then, it made sense to me, and I understood why I had been to these Eastern countries in my early life. I do recall the name of a town called Leipmeriz, in Czechoslovakia, a small apartment and an older lady dressed in black who sometimes must have babysat me. She would play tea time with me, and she sang songs in a beautiful language I did not understand. I remember calling her Babushka.

I also recall a time being in a horse-drawn carriage, traveling on a dirt road through some Eastern country with my father and mother. Suddenly, several men came out from the tall grasses and jumped onto the carriage with knives.

One of them was sitting high above me on the wagon, clipping his toenails, which hit my neck—strange memories. I remember my father giving them food, which they took and ran off with. They must have been harmless and hungry peasants.

Of my father, the memories are vague as well. Again, bits and pieces, images of a tall man in military uniform. Me sitting on his lap, sometimes screaming my head off to get away from his arms holding me too tight.

There was, I remember, a motorcycle with a sidecar in which I rode on my mother's lap, the wind blowing my hair and the two of them laughing. A few more memories of being at the train station in my hometown of Metz, perhaps when he would come home on leave. I was scared of him; my eyes were at the level of his high black boots, which made a lot of noise when he approached me. I remember the steam of the train encircling me in a gray cloud from which I tried to escape by burying my face in my mother's dress.

The first four years of my life were mostly filled with memories of the war. Air raid sirens blasting, bombs falling, spending many hours in our dark and damp cellar. Somehow, my child's mind made it a game when Opa would wake me in the middle of the night and carry me on his shoulders to the cellar.

I thought it was all in fun, especially with his gas mask on; he looked so funny. Once, I was told that Oma had covered me with her body as bricks and mortar fell all around us in the cellar. She sustained injuries to her back that lasted her a lifetime.

The next day, when we would go out to buy milk or bread, Oma would take me with her. The lines were endless and sometimes we would go home with nothing, not enough food for everyone. At times, I would see a body lying in the street, an arm or a leg. I thought they were tired people taking a nap. Thank God, a child does not always understand and is spared the horrors.

I would sometimes get in trouble during blackouts, when all windows at night were covered up with dark, heavy blankets to hide the lights from the outside. Only one or two candles would be lit in the kitchen. I would peek out the window and marvel at the colorful streaks of lights falling like rain, which I later found out were bombs. Or the spectacle of parachutes coming down like umbrellas. I don't remember feeling fear, but the sounds of sirens and bombs and the loud rumbling of fighter planes are still vivid in my memory to this day. I didn't suffer very much during those terrible times; it seemed to be a normal way of life. It wasn't until much later that I realized the psychological effects it can leave on a child forever.

At the age of eighteen months, I became ill with asthma and suffered from it until the age of sixteen. I can relate to what my father went through. It is a debilitating and scary illness. My attacks would last three or four days at a time. There was no medication in those days to bring relief. There were those terrible nights when I could not get enough air into my lungs and had to sit propped against pillows, unable to sleep.

I remember Oma sitting at my bedside for hours, holding my hand and comforting me. When the crisis was over, I would be weak for several days, my ribs killing me from the heavy breathing. This illness impacted my schooling a lot; I missed school for many days at a time. Therefore, I was not the best student and always fell behind. No one seemed to care, least of all me.

I started Catholic school at age five, and it was not among my favorite activities, especially with the sad grades I got. At that time, I did not know a single word of French and had to learn the hard way, since we only spoke German at home.

As I have already explained, some families had been lucky enough to leave the German-occupied provinces of Lorraine and Alsace to go to other parts of Southern France. When they returned after the war, they were fluent in French, which, of course, was not the case for me. However, children are fast learners. It took little time for me to speak as well as the others, and today I still speak fluently in both languages.

I still remember the first day of school. I had a brand-new satchel that contained a little slate board framed in wood; a box that held chalk, pencils, erasers, an ink pen, and a small ink bottle; and a notebook covered in dark blue paper with my name on it. It was my mother who took me the first day. I clung to her hand and did not want to enter the classroom where the other girls were already at their desks. A nun dressed in a long black robe and white hood took me to the end of the classroom and roughly sat me down. I unpacked my satchel and could not wait to get home, promising myself I would not come back the next day.

Days went by and I did go back to school; I had no choice. The drawback was that because my grandparents did not speak French, I had no help with my homework. Since I had to fend for myself, my schoolwork was never satisfactory, and I was constantly being punished by the teacher.

Because I was the daughter of a German SS officer, it was made clear to me that I was to never forget who I was and where I came from, and to speak only when spoken to. The nuns at school were extremely strict, and physical punishment was the norm and accepted in those days. Due to my frequent illnesses, I missed school a lot, and with no help at home with schoolwork, I was unable to keep up with the latest teachings.

Therefore, when called to recite a lesson or turn in some work, I was ill-prepared or not prepared at all. Being hit on the hands and legs with a ruler was the usual method of punishment. Sometimes my legs and fingers had large red welts on them that lasted for days, a way to show others what a poor student I was.

Somehow I became immune to punishments, and it was no use to complain at home. It was accepted as part of school discipline. When asked to the blackboard, I was ordered to click my heels and salute Hitler in front of the class; it was so humiliating. Posture was a big thing, and if we were caught slouching over our desks, a stick was placed inside our clothes along our back to hold us straight.

I loved writing poems and reading, but Oma would get very upset if she caught me. To her, it was a waste of time. She would compare me to my father, who loved writing—the good-for-nothing, the killer, the enemy, as she called him. I did not understand the hatred and wondered who this man was that caused such negativity.

31
CHRISTA

When I turned seven, I met my very first friend. Christa was her name. She also was the daughter of a German SS officer. Her father had been killed during the war, and sadly, her mother had died in a car accident when Christa was two years old. Like me, she was raised by her grandparents. We bonded and were always together. We had a lot in common and stood up to the mockeries of the other girls, who called us Krauts.

A year later, we were to make our first communion, a big celebration in our Catholic faith.

A week before our communion, tragedy struck. It was May 20, 1949.

After dinner on nice days, Opa and Oma would always take an evening walk. That day, we walked along a busy road in Christa's neighborhood. She was out in her front yard, and she saw us and called my name as she crossed the road. We hugged, and after a few words she crossed the road back to her house.

All I remember are terrible sounds of screeching brakes and tires, my Oma screaming.

I saw her little body in the middle of the road; she had been struck by a truck. I don't remember much after that. She died that night at 1:30 a.m. It was so ironic that her mom had died a few years earlier, hit by a car. To this day, I blame myself for having been there at that time that evening.

Figure16.   Christa was tragically killed in May 1949.

The day of my communion, which was to be such a happy and bright day, turned out to be one of the saddest. I sat in church, tears streaking down my face. Christa should have been sitting at my side. But, she was gone forever.

Her funeral was held a couple of days later. My grandparents did not let me attend; perhaps they thought it would be too hard on me. I went to school that day so terribly alone and sad. Her seat next to mine was empty, and I kept looking at the door as if, by a miracle, she would appear. No one seemed to notice or even care. The teacher never made any mention of it.

In the fall of that same year, I was no longer accepted at school. My grandparents were told I was a bad influence on the other children, with my German accent and my father's history.

A new school accepted me; it was a public school. No more nuns. But I could have cared less.

I decided to never depend on anyone, never need anyone,

and never love anyone again.

However, the new school turned out to be better than the last one. The new crowd of girls seemed to like me. I was not called names or made fun of for a change. I started lying and telling stories, told them that my father was dead. No one questioned anything. But again, I didn't get to stay longer than a few months and was asked to leave for the same reasons as before. I was a KRAUT.

Figure17. My Mother and little cousin Lydia with me on my Communion May 29, 1949.

32
GEORGETTE

I have to go back in time a little.

Georgette was my youngest aunt, my mother's sister. She was only eleven years older than me. When I was almost five years old, she gave birth to a baby. Georgette was then sixteen years old, and had met and fallen in love with a Bosnian soldier named Branko Uzkanina. However, he had to return to the front lines shortly after they met. Two months later, Georgette found out she was pregnant. When they parted, he gave her his word to come back for her when the war was over. He also gave her a medal of St. Christopher that he wore around his neck, as a promise. A medal his mother had given him as a child.

She waited and waited for news of him, but none ever came. Heartbroken, she believed he had been killed and put the medal around her newborn baby girl's neck. However, as she would find out many years later, he did write her. She never received those letters; Oma burned them as they arrived. Oma wanted her daughter to have nothing to do with another foreigner; my father was enough for that family.

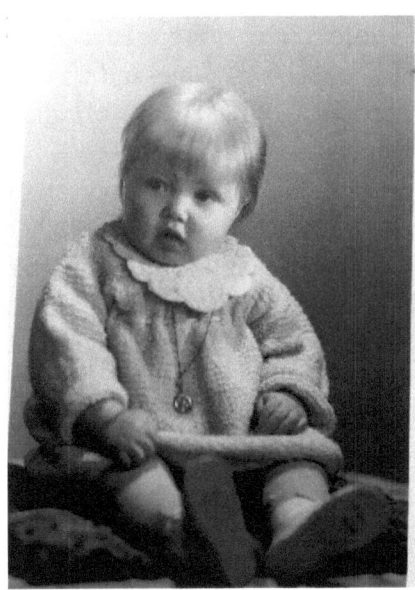

Lydia was a beautiful child with big brown eyes, and later, the longest blond hair. Georgette went on with her young life but never forgot Branko. My grandparents raised the baby as they had done with me. We grew up together like sisters. I adored her.

Two years later, Georgette met a French soldier, Pierre. They married, but Lydia never went to live with him. She stayed with Oma and Opa. Sadly, Georgette and her daughter never bonded, no more than my mother and I had. For Lydia and me, Oma and Opa were our parents.

Figure18. Lydia. Georgette and Branko's Daughter

Figure19. Branko Uzkanina, Lydia's Father.

Seventeen years later, a letter arrived from Paris with Georgette's name. Sender unknown to my Oma, and written in French. It came from a woman by the name of Miranda Koslovski. Oma asked me to translate the letter.

Georgette and I had always been close. We were only eleven years apart in age and shared a lot. She had told me about her first love. How they had met in 1944, and found out after his departure that she had gotten pregnant. She never heard of him after he went back to the front lines and thought he had been killed.

The letter said he had never heard from her since they had parted and was inquiring if she had survived the war. Oma immediately took the letter from me and tore it up. Made me swear to never mention a word about it to Georgette, not even to Opa. I still had the envelope and address in my hand and put it in my pocket, unnoticed by Oma.

A few days later, I saw Georgette and told her about the letter from Paris. She broke down in tears and could not believe that Branko was alive. Here it was seventeen years later—she was married with five children and Branko was alive.

She confronted her parents, told them she knew about Branko. I was present during the confrontation. It was an ugly one and Oma turned on me severely. Opa told her he had nothing to do with it, and Oma admitted she had not wanted her young daughter involved with a foreign soldier much too old for her. She told her she had destroyed all the letters. I still remember the screams and cries; Georgette accused her mother of having destroyed her life. She had married without love only to be accepted by family and society.

She contacted the woman in Paris and asked for Branko's address. A few weeks later, she found the courage to write him. He still lived in Bosnia. She told him she had never heard from him and was now married with children. He wrote back, told her he had never forgotten her in all those years. He also had married, but had no children. He was to go to Paris on business in a few weeks and asked if he could stop by Metz, her hometown, so they could see each other one last time. She agreed.

They were to meet at a little restaurant in town for lunch. Georgette was a nervous wreck, could find nothing suitable to wear, thought herself old and ugly. Would he even recognize the young schoolgirl he had fallen in love with so long ago? At the very last moment, she decided against going; she could not go through with it.

A few days later, she received a letter. He had waited two hours before taking the train back to his country. Why had she not come? Her response was that she had lost courage and that it would be preferable to keep the memories of each other as they were then, young and in love.

She told him about her marriage and children, but never once told him about their child, Lydia.

They promised to stay in touch with a letter once a year around Christmastime. For ten years, they kept their promise; each year a letter was exchanged. He still had no children but was happy in his marriage. Then, one year, there was no letter from him, and none the following year, or the ones after that.

A couple of years later, when I returned for a visit to France, I went to see Georgette right away. She looked so different and so sad; she refused to talk about Branko. Made me swear to never tell Lydia about him and what I knew. She said she had a dream that he had died. This time she said she knew he was gone forever.

I saw Georgette each time I returned to France over the years. Never did Branko's name come up.

She passed away in 2007, in her mid-seventies. But, before passing, she finally told her daughter the truth about her real father. Lydia and her mom had never been close; there was little mother–daughter relationship. Lydia never forgave her for having kept the heavy secret all those years.

Lydia did some research about her father and found out he had lived all his life in Bosnia, but had passed away several years ago.

Lydia died October 13, 2017, at age seventy-two, of leukemia and heart failure. To the very end, she had been unable to forgive her mother.

Figure 20.   Lydia.

33
CÉCILE

Then there was my other aunt Cécile, the eldest of the three sisters. She was also my godmother.

At age eighteen, she left home for Paris to join a well-known dancing cabaret known as the Folies Bergère as a chorus girl. The escape did not last very long. When Opa, her father, found out where she was, he went immediately to Paris and, in the middle of a show, pulled her off the stage, to her great embarrassment. One can only imagine the scene—a half-naked dancer in feathers and glitter, pulled off the stage by an irate father. In those days, one had to be twenty-one to be emancipated.

However, she had fallen in love with the director of the cabaret. A few weeks later, he came to ask for her hand in marriage. They were married six months later, and she returned to Paris with him. The marriage lasted only five years, with no children. She remarried a few years later, had two children and left her dancing career behind. She became a renowned seamstress in our hometown and made my first ballroom gown of pink satin, which I wore at my coming-out ball when I turned eighteen.

When I was in kindergarten, I loved when she picked me up after school. She was always dressed in the latest fashion and smelled of the best perfumes. And as a bonus, she gave me my first dance lessons when I turned sixteen. I always greatly admired her and wanted to follow in her footsteps.

She actually entered me in a dance contest when I turned eighteen. It was a seventeen-hour tango marathon and I won first place. I was paired with a talented gentleman from São Paulo. We made a wonderful team. I never saw him again after the competition and was unable to enjoy the first prize, a trip to the French Riviera for one week at a beautiful resort. Oma put a stop to it immediately when she found out. She even shredded the only newspaper photo I had of my once-in-a-lifetime success. I was a disgrace in her eyes, no better than Cécile, her daughter. But it was too late. I had dancing in the blood and adored my godmother, Cécile, with whom I had a great relationship throughout my growing-up years. She was always there for me when I needed to talk or wanted advice.

She passed away in her late seventies and left a great void in my life.

Figure21. From right: My Mother, Opa, Oma, and my Aunt Cécile.

Let's get back to my earlier days at Oma and Opa's.

My favorite place was the attic. I loved the smell of old wood up there. Through the rooftop windows, I could see the countryside far away. There were old worn-out trunks made of wood and metal, full of ancient musty-smelling clothes, dishes, books and old photo albums that made me wonder who had once owned them. People long gone, perhaps. It was my hideaway; no one ever thought of looking for me up there, and I was free to write and dream.

In Europe, our windows have no screens and one can lean out, watch people passing by, greet them and chitchat. I would often sit at the windows of our living room on Saturday nights when I was only seven or eight years old, listening to the sounds of an accordion coming from a small outdoor café in the distance.

The waltzes and tangos made me dream of the days I would go dancing. I think I learned how to dance in my head long before I knew on my feet.

We lived outside of the city, in a place where shepherds sometimes still herded back the sheep in the fall.

There was a milk store, a butcher shop, a bakery, a couple of small grocery stores and a shoemaker. Everyone knew everyone, and it was a safe place to live. The church up on the hill was beautiful, a few centuries old, and had suffered minor damage from the war.

Then overnight my life changed. In 1950, life as I knew it came to an abrupt end and so did my childhood.

Figure22. The Mailman still delivered on his bycicle.

34
THE HUNGRY YEARS

We are what happened to us. We carry everywhere all that has shaped us, all that we lacked, all that we wanted and never got, all that we got but never wanted, all that was found and lost.

– Douglas Kennedy

I was nine years old. One day when I came home from school, my mother was there, which was most unusual. The atmosphere was somber; I guessed immediately that something was wrong and it had to do with me. In a corner of the kitchen was a suitcase with some of my belongings on top of it.

I looked at my Opa, who had his back turned and was looking out the window. Oma was crying. I ran and clung to her; she hugged me tight and I still remember what she said.

"You have to go with your mother. She has remarried and wants her family back together. Your little brother, Jean-Pierre, will join you in a few days. We have no legal rights over you. She is your mother."

I could not believe what I heard and started screaming at my mother, how I did not want to go with her, how I did not love her and she had no right to take me away. No amount of tears and screaming did any good. She shook me, told me it was not my choice but hers. Grabbed my suitcase and pushed me out of the apartment. I looked back at Oma and Opa, screaming and crying. They did not move, just stood there with the saddest look on their faces. I never felt so lost.

And so started my new life.

74 RUE DU PONTIFFROY.

Figure 23. The front entrance.

This was the street address where I would live for the next six years. It was in the worst neighborhood of the city of Metz, a slum area.

The building my mother lived in was on the third floor of a run-down apartment that looked worse than the streets. The photos I have were given to me years later by an uncle who was an amateur photographer in his day. This neighborhood no longer exists. It was demolished in the late 1980s.

Hesitantly, I entered the apartment. There was a small kitchen with a double bed standing in a corner, surrounded by a heavy dark green curtain for privacy. I guessed it was my mother and her husband's bed. A cement sink was at the other end of the room, with some mushrooms growing on the ceiling above because of a leak from the roof. A table stood at the center of the room with a vase of fresh flowers, such a contrast with the dinginess of the place.

There was a small buffet and a gas stove next to it. Only a portion of gray sky could be seen through the room's two small windows.

Across the courtyard, almost in arm's reach, was another dirty run-down building. It was so dark in that room it gave me shivers. My mother showed me the bedroom, and what a bedroom it was.

By today's standards, it would be no larger or longer than a walk-in closet.

Figure24. The two small windows at the top looked out from the apartment.

There were three beds and a small dresser, over which hung two framed pictures, one of Jesus and one of Mary. At the end of the narrow room was a very tiny window, from which I could see only a piece of sky, the run-down building across from us, and a row of crows sitting on the rooftop, screaming their heads off.

Oh, God! How I wanted to cry, but my throat was so tight I couldn't. I just stood there frozen like a statue. My mother removed my coat, took me back to the kitchen and seated me on a chair.

"We will be happy together, you'll see. Tonight you will meet your new father and his little girl. She is still a baby. You are now nine years old, old enough to help me take care of her and your brother, Jean-Pierre, who will arrive in a couple of days. He is living with a family in the country. Now I want my children together and to have a family life." No sound came out of my dry mouth. All I could think about was running away. All I could see was that sad environment in which I was now to live.

Why did my grandparents allow this? Why did they abandon me? Why did they let me go to this woman I did not know or like? This stranger!

Later in the evening, a man walked in, and my mother threw herself in his arms. "Annita is here," she said.

She pushed me toward him and I felt immediate fear and disgust. He smelled of alcohol and tobacco. "Look what we have here," he said, staring at me. "That will be great for you, Marceline. She can help you with the household and the kids."

In his arms, he held a little girl. She was perhaps three years old, with blond hair that looked as if it had not been combed or washed for a while. She seemed very shy and kept her eyes down. Her name was Yolanda.

That night in bed, the tears finally came. I sobbed and sobbed. I was so lonely for my grandparents, so scared, so frightened. I wanted my Oma and Opa, their arms around me, my bed at home, my safe haven. I had to smother my cries to avoid waking Yolanda, who was asleep in her little bed next to mine.

I must eventually have fallen asleep because it was already morning when I opened my eyes. A gray, rainy morning. My mother took me to a school that day to sign me up. I was to start the following week. Again changes, a new school, new kids and teachers.

Jean-Pierre, my unknown brother, arrived two days later. He was almost five years old, with blond hair, slanted blue eyes, and a sweet smile. I loved him right away and he must have sensed it, as he came straight to me, took my hand in his and snuggled at my side. Now there were three of us in that small bedroom, but it strangely felt more comforting and less lonely with the two little ones there. I heard Jean-Pierre cry in the middle of the night. I went to him, and he snuggled, sucking his two middle fingers. I remember him asking me not to leave him because he was scared. I slipped into bed next to him, his head on my shoulder, and felt his tears. Finally he relaxed, and I heard his soft breathing. Only then did I fall asleep.

I hated my new school right away. It was a public school and the teachers were just as severe as the nuns had been. I figured I would be expelled soon anyway when they found out I was the daughter of an SS officer. It was no use to make friends or even bother getting good grades. But, to my surprise, the girls were very nice and soon I had two good friends, Christiane and Paulette, who both lived in the same neighborhood. However, I had little time to go out and play. My mother was gone from morning to late in the evening most days, and sometimes all night as well. I thought she worked, but soon found out that she spent her days and nights in bars and pubs.

The two little ones were hanging on to me all the time. I could not leave them alone in the apartment to meet my new friends. I was nine years old and responsible for them. I loved my little brother a lot; although he had never been part of my life, we bonded immediately. He had a sweet disposition—shy, loving, never demanded much—and I made sure he had plenty of playtime with the little boys in the neighborhood. I loved combing his blond hair with the little curly lock falling over his right eye.

Yolanda, on the other hand, was very withdrawn and would sit for hours in her playpen, just holding onto an old rag doll. Always looking down, never making eye contact. Although she was three, she had to stay in her playpen a lot. It was the only safe place for her when she was left alone while my brother and I were at school. I supposed my mother must have come home during the day to check on her and feed her. The only enjoyment I saw in her eyes was when I bathed her once a week in a metal bucket, when we had enough warm water. Those were the only times I would see a smile on that little face, but I never heard her laugh.

More and more often, my mother was absent. The few times she was home were a blessing; it was when she did not drink and would cook dinner for us, which was seldom. Only then could I go out and play with my two friends for an hour or two. Those opportunities became less frequent as time went on. Sometimes, she and her husband would be gone for three days at a time. I had no idea where they were.

I had to find food for the three of us, and stealing in stores became the norm. I would teach Jean-Pierre to fill his pockets while I talked to the grocer, who refused to give me credit for food. My mother owed him too much already. Same with the bakery and the milk store. At times, Jean-Pierre could manage to steal a couple of eggs, a small loaf of bread, a candy or two. I did the same, hiding behind customers in order not to be seen. I would fill my pockets and coat sleeves with whatever I could put my hands on, then quietly leave the store, my heart pounding. Sometimes we would look into trash cans and be lucky to find something decent, like a half-rotten apple, an orange, or some dry bread. It did not matter to us, we were so hungry. One who has never known real hunger has no clue what it feels like. The pain in the stomach doubles you over, and anything you can put in your mouth is a blessing. That's how we made it most of the time.

In the morning, I would warm up some leftover coffee or some water and cut up stale bread in it with a little sugar. That was breakfast most days. Jean-Pierre, years later, remembered those breakfasts as his favorite ones. Then, I would dress Yolanda and Jean-Pierre, put the little girl back in her playpen with a bottle of sugar water, and take my brother to school.

Yolanda was left alone until we returned from school around four o'clock in the afternoon.

The place would smell of urine. Yolanda would go without a diaper change for the longest time. I would wash the diapers the best I could and hang them out the window to dry. The poor child had sores on her little bottom but never complained. Most of the time, she was like a lifeless doll, never needing anything, just letting herself be handled and fed. Always with the sad little face of an unloved child. Her mother had died of lung disease when Yolanda was a year and a half old. She had stayed with her grandparents, but I have no clue what her baby years were like until her father married my mother.

I don't have a single picture of us together, only memories.

She had one cloth doll, dirty, ripped, with few hairs left, but she clung to it at all times. It was the only thing that must have represented security, and the only comfort she had.

The nights were the worst, when my mother and her husband would come home drunk and fight.

The fights were horrible—screams and blows, dishes crashing and furniture overturned. It became a habit for me to run away in the middle of the night in my slippers and nightgown to go to Oma and Opa's, an hour away on foot.

I don't know how I made it through the city streets at night and did not come to harm. I would run through dark streets, away from the main thoroughfare, in fear of running into a policeman or the many North Africans who roamed the street in those days. Perhaps I had a guardian angel looking over me.

However, I could never stay with my grandparents. The next day, Opa would take me back on his bicycle, which he loaded with food for us. Oma would hug me with tears in her eyes and explain that my mother had legal rights and I could no longer stay with them. My heart would be so heavy, but I knew I would be back the first chance I had.

Christiane, the little friend who lived on my street, was always there for me. Her parents owned a bar and restaurant where my mother hung out a lot. However, there was not much time for me to play, with the two young ones needing me constantly.

Besides, I had no toys of my own like the other kids my age. Christiane would loan me her roller skates sometimes, or her bicycle. I would race up and down the street at a dangerous speed, enjoying the thrill. I hated my life and missed my real home so very much. But it was only the beginning of six long and miserable years. Years that would be ghosts of painful memories for my entire life.

One day, my mother brought home a lost puppy she had found roaming the streets. I loved him at first sight, called him Rexi and claimed him as mine. He was a Japanese Spitz, all fluffy white with big black eyes. My mother said I could have him if I took care of him and fed him. You bet I would take care of him and feed him. I would just have to find more food.

At night he would sleep with me, and in the morning he would follow my brother and me to school.

I don't know where he went during the day, but every afternoon at four o'clock, he would faithfully be waiting for us in front of the school gates. All the kids knew him, loved him and gave him treats. He was my buddy and I could not have loved him more.

One day, when he was about four years old, I came out of school and Rexi was not there. No Rexi waiting for me. Fear gripped my heart—did he get run over? Did someone take him away?

My brother and I roamed the street for hours looking for him, calling him, asking people, but in vain. No one had seen Rexi. Nighttime came and Rexi had not returned. My mother did not come home until early the next morning, drunk as usual and belligerent. Later that day, she explained they gave Rexi to a farmer and that he would be happier, with plenty of food and space to roam. She said he was only another mouth to feed anyway. I cried for days, begged her to please get him back. I would do anything she asked of me—clean the house, take better care of the kids—but it did no good. Rexi never came back. I did not even have the chance to hold him and say goodbye. How I hated these two people.

A few months later, I found out the truth—he never went to a farmer. My mother and her husband had drowned him in the river nearby. I hated her even more from that moment on. Dear God, how I hated them both, how could they have been so cruel. I cried for days on end, walked the edges of the river in the hope he had survived and perhaps someone had saved him. It was just wishful thinking, and deep in my heart I knew he was gone; I would never hold and love my Rexi again.

35
INHUMANITY

My schoolwork suffered more and more as time went on. I was not a great student, my grades were terrible, and I had no desire to study—who cared anyway! The sadness would not lift and I cried myself asleep most nights. So ironic that many years later, when I read my father's journal, I found out about his dog Bubby, his tragic ending and what my father felt when he lost him. How I understood his pain.

I did a little babysitting in the evenings for a little boy about nine months old. I guess his mother hung out with mine. I made a little money, enough to go to a movie once a month on Thursday afternoons when we had no school.

I selfishly would not share with anyone. I left Yolanda and Jean-Pierre at home for a couple of hours on those days, told my brother he was in charge until I got back and would bring them a candy or two. It was my only escape.

I was ten years old when my girlfriend Christiane had an appendectomy and was in the hospital for two weeks. In those days, one stayed a lot longer under medical care. I envied how much attention she received from the kids at school and from her family. My mother even talked about her. Her mom went to the hospital daily, and at school we would draw pictures for her.

I got a splendid idea and started complaining of a sharp pain on the right side of my abdomen. That's where Christiane had told me it hurt. My mom told me it was gas and to use the pot more often. But I did not give up and continued complaining. After three days, she took me seriously and called a doctor who did home visits in the evenings, as was customary in those days. He told her it was my appendix and wanted to hospitalize me for surgery.

I was in seventh heaven to see my mother worry and have her hold me in her arms, something so unusual. Now, I would finally be loved more, I figured. She would visit me in the hospital every day and I would be the talk of the school. I would be spoiled, and would no longer have to clean the house and take care of the kids.

She took me to the hospital the next day. I was scheduled for 10:00 a.m. My mother kissed me goodbye and hugged me so tight I could hardly breathe.

She told me she would be back after the surgery. I was so happy for the first time in a very long time. I felt loved and important in her eyes.

The nurses came with a gurney to take me to the operating block. Now fear struck. I started crying and told the nurses that I had lied. I never had any pain. They tried to calm me down, saying my mom would be here when I got back to the room.

When I woke up in my hospital bed, my mouth was terribly dry and my head hurt. A nurse sitting next to me put a wet sponge on my lips. My mom was not there. I started crying and fell back asleep. I stayed fourteen days, waited and waited for my mom each day, but she never came. My Opa and Oma came almost every day but did not know where my mother was. There were five other children in the room and I felt a little less lonely. Also, there was a little boy my age who would sit at my side, tell me stories and sing songs to me. His parents would sometimes bring me oranges or candies. During those days, I often wondered how Yolanda and Jean-Pierre were getting along.

On the day of my discharge, my mother came early in the morning, hugged me as if nothing had happened and signed me out, and we left the hospital. She took me to a park nearby, sat me on a bench, gave me an apple and told me to wait here. She had an errand to run and would be right back.

It was a sunny, warm day. I watched the birds, squirrels, and pigeons all around me. The sun felt so good on my face after those long, dark days at the hospital. I sat there, waited and waited with my apple in my lap. I felt like crying but held back.

Hours went by; it was probably late afternoon and she had not returned. A policeman came over to me while I was half-asleep on the bench, hungry and tired. He had seen me sitting there for several hours and asked my name and what I was doing there. I explained I was waiting for my mom and that I was not to go anywhere until she returned.

He was a very nice man, who gently took me by the hand and walked me to the police department. It was now 6:00 p.m. and I had sat there since 11:00 a.m.

I totally forget how the situation ended. I must have blocked it out of my mind. To this day, I have no recollection other than knowing I had not been loved as I had hoped. I had done it all in vain.

And so life resumed its normalcy, if it can be called that. Jean-Pierre and Yolanda were so happy to see me. Yolanda cuddled in my arms for the first time, and my little brother questioned me over and over about my stay at the hospital and said how he had envied me. Poor kid, little did he know.

Not long after that, my mother told me I had to help out more and that she had found me a job at a florist's shop where I would work as a delivery girl after school. I was ten years old.

I worked there daily until sometimes 8:00 p.m. I would deliver flowers to customers, collect the money in cash and turn it in to my boss the next day. When I got tips (very seldom), my mother took the money from me.

It was not a terrible job, and I almost liked it, except on rainy or cold days. My bosses would always give me a sandwich, which I so appreciated.

One evening, I felt ill and started having an asthma attack, which happened frequently. I must have had a high fever as well; I was shaking and could not wait to go home to bed. I went home with the money I had collected that evening in my coat pocket.

It was late October and raining; I was drenched. When I got home, the children were alone. I was too weak and sick to cook and care for them that night. I gave Yolanda and Jean-Pierre a bottle of sugar water and some bread, then went to bed. Jean-Pierre, poor little guy, stayed at my side and held my hand. The next day I had a high fever. I did not go to school, or to work that evening, nor the day after.

The florist, who had not heard from me, contacted my mother and asked for his money. I told her it was in my coat pocket. She looked and said there was no money and accused me of stealing it. I could not believe my ears. Did it fall out? It could not have; I knew it had been where I put it. Of course, I was fired. A few days later, Jean-Pierre told me he had seen our mom go through my coat pockets and take something out.

My grandparents paid the florist, but he did not want me back.

My mother found me another job a couple of weeks later, evenings after school again, at a grocery store, stacking and unpacking boxes and cleaning floors. I held the job for six months, but I was sick a lot and had to miss work. Of course I was fired. But I was happy about that; I hated the job and missed out on so much. The only benefit was that I had been able to fill my pockets with some much-needed food for the children and had never been caught.

One night, the children and I were awakened by what sounded like a baby screaming. The screaming became unbearable, as if the child were hurt, and it lasted what seemed a long time until finally silence came. I covered my head with my pillow; Yolanda was crying her head off with fear. I took her into my bed and soon Jean-Pierre joined us. All cramped together, we felt safer until we finally fell asleep.

The next morning when I got up, my mother was home cleaning the linoleum floor. There were red spots all over. I asked where the baby was, and she said, "What baby? Where did you get this idea from?" I really thought nothing more of it and went off to school. That night she was home cooking dinner, a rabbit stew, such a treat for us. Albert came home drunk as usual, but not in a bad mood for a change.

We ate and he asked, laughing out loud, how we liked the cat stew. I did not understand. He said, "The cat we found in the street last night and skinned alive." I almost vomited and remembered the red spots on the floor that morning and the terrible screams we had heard the night before.

Then, to my horror, he pointed at two bloody strings hanging from the wooden ceiling beam. To this day, I can still hear those horrible screams I had mistaken for a baby's cry. My God! They had skinned an animal alive, a cat. What monsters were these two people? How could they have been so cruel, so inhuman?

36
SIX YEARS

Life continued. The months went by, so very, very slow, and I was lonely.

One night, the children and I were in bed. As usual, no adults were home.

Around 10:00 p.m. or so, I heard Albert staggering up the stairs, but I did not hear my mother's footsteps.

He was in the kitchen for a while, moving things around, walking back and forth, and then he left again. I had an uneasy feeling and got up to see what he had done in the kitchen, but noticed nothing unusual and went back to bed. What woke me up next were loud voices, someone grabbing me out of bed and carrying me downstairs. I faintly heard Yolanda crying; it sounded far away and I felt so tired.

When I woke up again, I was in bed at my aunt Georgette's house, and I later found out Albert had tried to kill us by turning on the gas stove. Drunk, he had gone to my uncle and aunt's house and told them that the children were dead.

My uncle and aunt rushed over and saved our lives just in time. How much longer would it have been before the gas had done its job and—who knows, blown up the entire building? Where was our mother? Drunk somewhere, as usual? Nothing was ever reported to the police or social services, and life continued as usual. Except that from that moment on, I was always afraid I would fall asleep and not wake up.

It seemed that no one was looking into the situation with my mother and the monster Albert.

My grandparents were helpless and had contacted social services several times, but they were told they needed proof and no one had reported anything. Strange times we lived in, in the 1950s—didn't anyone care about abused children? It was the norm in that sordid neighborhood.

Meanwhile, I continued to be frequently bedridden with asthma attacks. It was terrible not to be able to breathe and so scary to be alone with this. No one was there to comfort me, my mother never took it too seriously, and there was no medication to help in those days. I so missed my grandmother at my side, holding my hand and wiping my forehead.

Little Yolanda, now five years old, was her father's scapegoat. He never put a hand on my brother or me—the little one took all the blows. It was as if he hated the child. She was so little and defenseless, there was nothing I could do to protect her. At least she now went to kindergarten and seemed to be happier.

Sometimes he would make her stand in a corner of the kitchen with a paper bag over her head. This would sometimes last for thirty minutes or more. Her little legs would tremble. If she tried to go to her knees, he would whip her with his belt. Or, at times, he would have her stare at a photo of her dead mother. A dead woman lying on a bed, hands crossed over a rosary. This was so cruel. She was too young to understand, and would just look at the photo without knowing who the woman was.

One day, though, I stood up to him. I was perhaps twelve years old then. He was beating my mother; she was almost unconscious on the kitchen floor with cuts to her head and lips.

He kept beating and beating her with his fists. I grabbed a tall bottle of beer from the kitchen table, held it high above my head and moved toward him, locking my eyes with his. Strangely, I felt no fear as I continued approaching him. He raised his fist and came toward me. I swore I saw fear in his eyes. He came so close I smelled his alcoholic breath, and my legs started shaking.

Then he lowered his fist and said, "You're not worth it." Then he walked out of the apartment. From that moment on, I knew I would never fear him again, or anyone else. I knew I would never ever let a man lay a hand on me; I could be hurt, but I would always fight back. I looked at my pitiful mother on the floor and swore to never be like her.

Seeing all this misery, living this terrible life, made me stronger and taught me to always fight for what I believed in. Perhaps this horrible life was not all in vain after all.

Of those six years, I have but a single good memory. It was Christmas Eve, and I was thirteen years old. Albert and my mother had put up a Christmas tree, the only one we ever had while living with them all those years. Usually, on Christmas Eve, the three of us roamed the streets from bar to bar, looking for our mother. We were always envious of the Christmas trees we saw through windows at other homes, and of the happy laughter of families that we heard as we walked the cold streets.

Those sights and sounds made us feel abandoned and very lonely. I would hold the little ones' hands, repress my tears, and sing them Christmas songs I had learned from Oma and Opa.

But that particular Christmas was different for whatever reason. My mother and Albert were home and sober. There was a decorated tree in the kitchen corner, the smell of food and, wonder of wonders, some gifts under the tree. For me, there was a doll with red curly hair and eyelids that opened and closed. I loved her immediately, and my mother suggested I call her Dora. These days, a doll would not be something a girl would want at age thirteen. But those were such different times. We had no television, no electronic gadgets and no books to read, and we were happy with very little.

I loved my doll; I never had such a nice one in my entire life. For me, she was the most wonderful gift in the world. There was also a doll for Yolanda and a train set for my brother.

We were in paradise that night. Why could it not be like this always, a mom and dad at home and the smell of food?

In those days, I still had Rexi. He hated to share a spot in bed with me and Dora and would growl at her; it was so funny. One day, however, he decided to chew off Dora's hands. I was devastated. My mother, to my astonishment, took her to a repairman, where she stayed for six months until I saved enough money to pay for the repair. It was during those six months that I lost Rexi. I was lonelier than ever—no Rexi, no Dora in whom to confide my deepest thoughts and secrets at night.

I had managed to save money from my little side jobs. No candies, no movies anymore—I needed Dora back. When she returned, she had new hands. However, they were paler than the rest of her body, which was a darker pink. It did not matter; I had her back and was no longer so lonely.

37
THE END OF THE NIGHTMARE

When I came to live with my mother, she was about twenty-nine years old. I didn't know at the time that she was already ill with tuberculosis. All I knew was her strong need for alcohol and cigarettes.

As the years went on, it was awful to hear her cough and see her spit blood into her handkerchief. I had no idea of the seriousness of her disease and how dangerous for us children it was. I remember her passing out sometimes when she could not breathe and blood filled her mouth. I would wipe her face and hold her hand, frightened at the sight of the blood. But she would bounce back as if nothing were wrong. As time went on, I also noticed she was losing weight and her clothes would hang on her frame. She was sick and vomited a lot. Again, I did not know what was going on, and it did not seem like a big deal at that time in my life.

My health kept getting worse; I lost weight, had no appetite, and missed school more and more. When I was almost fourteen, the director of the school reported it to social services; I guess that's how they finally got involved.

Jean-Pierre, now almost ten years old, was doing all he could to find more food. He was good at bringing home cheese or bread. Poor little guy, I felt so bad for him but was myself too ill and helpless to do anything.

Yolanda, now seven, would often stay at my side and silently hold my hand. I will always remember her sad little face while she would sing songs to please me. I loved her so dearly and never forgot those difficult but precious moments. She never called me by my name, but always addressed me as her big sister.

Shortly before my fourteenth birthday, social services paid us a visit. Two very kind ladies came to the apartment when I was alone with the children. They asked about our parents, said they would be back the next day and requested that they be present. When they returned, only my mother was there. They questioned her and us about our lifestyle, gave my mother food coupons, and told her they would check in once a week.

My uncle Pierre, who was my aunt Georgette's husband, would sometimes pay a visit to my mother. He was a cook at a military base and would bring leftover food every once in a while.

One day, I was home with the children when he came to drop off some soup. He asked to talk to me alone in the bedroom. I had a strange sense of uneasiness, and I was right. He pushed me onto the bed; I screamed for him to get away from me and kicked as hard as I could. I don't know what stopped him. Perhaps the proximity of the children in the next room. He slapped me hard in the face and left.

I ran sobbing to my aunt's house to tell her what had happened. As I was ready to ring the doorbell, Pierre walked up behind me. He grabbed me by the neck, told me that if I said anything to my aunt, he would come back to beat me up. I ran away crying and never dared tell anyone.

Two weeks later, the women from social services came again. Mother was not home, as usual.

They were gentle with us, told us to get our coats and a favorite toy for the little ones and, without explanation, took us with them. We walked to the center of the city and entered a large building that looked like a school; it was the Child Welfare Agency. Children of all ages were playing in a courtyard.

We were told our mother would be along shortly, but in the meantime we had to be separated according to ages. Yolanda held my hand, screaming. They had to pry her away from me; her eyes begged me not to let her go. To this day, I remember the anguish in her face and the tears.

I started to run after her, but someone held me back and told me it would only be for a short time. Then they took Jean-Pierre. He let go of my hand and looked up at me with tears in his eyes.

I gave him a big hug and told him we would be back together in a little while, that mother was on her way. He stared at me and waved goodbye as they took him away. Not a sound came from his lips. I could not understand what was going on—surely our mother would come any time now to take us home. Little did I know at that moment that years would pass before I saw my brother again, much less that I would never, ever see Yolanda again.

That night I slept in a large dormitory with other girls, a place for homeless children where I stayed for one long week. Mother never came. I wondered how my brother and little Yolanda were doing. When I asked, I was told, "In time you will see them." I was examined by a doctor, who said I would need treatment for my asthma. I would be sent to a medical facility in the mountains where the climate would be better for me. I asked daily about the little ones and was given the same answer over and over: They were fine and not to worry.

Later, I also found out that my grandparents knew nothing of our predicament until I was already at a treatment center in the high French Alps, in a little town called Chamonix where I stayed for one year. I loved every minute of it, everything about it, and had never been happier. The town was surrounded by beautiful snowcapped mountains, there was fresh air and daily food, and I started thriving health-wise. I made lots of new friends for the first time in my life, and my grades at school went up.

The first six weeks I was on total bed rest, then little by little I could go outside and walk in the huge park on the property before being allowed longer mountain walks. Soon I was at the head of my class, and nobody called me a Kraut or knew about my childhood. My most wonderful and happy days were in that beautiful little mountain town. To this day, my memories of the place are the fondest and most unforgettable. It was my healing place. I never heard one word from my mother since social services had taken us away. My grandparents came to visit a couple of times. It was an eleven-hour train ride for them.

But eventually, the year came to an end and it was time for me to go home. Home?? Where? Back to my mother? I did not want to go back to her and that miserable way of life. There hadn't been a word from my little brother or Yolanda; daily they had been on my mind. It was as if I had been cut off from everything. But to my greatest joy, I found out that my mother had lost her maternal rights and that my grandparents had custody of me. I would go home, my real home, the one I grew up in and where I had been loved. I couldn't have been happier.

My grandparents came to take me home. We took the little mountain train down to the main station of St Gervais. I stood out on the platform, tears clouding my eyes as I saw my mountains fade away.

I saw Jean-Pierre once or twice after my return to Metz. He was still at the orphanage.

I wanted nothing to do with my mother and did not see her for at least two years after my return from Chamonix. My life with her was miles away now, and I can earnestly say that those awful years with her had made me stronger and more self-reliant. Yolanda had been placed out of town, I have no idea where.

I weaved happiness and sadness together over the years into the fabric of who I am today. But I never forgot where I came from. I learned we cannot change our destiny, but that we can control and shape it. Even when confronted with tragedies and sorrows, we can choose to be swallowed by it or to move on. I was now happy again and back home to my wonderful, loving grandparents, and I had dreams of going to nursing school. The future was full of promise.

I read somewhere that we cannot always choose the music life plays, but we can choose how we dance to it.

Figure 25. Brother, Jean-Pierre, Age 18.

38
YOUNG LIONS

Over the years, I have wondered who my mother was. Who was this woman, never there for her children, who lived a life of debauchery? What was her childhood like? Who was little Marceline during those terrible war years? How did she grow up, and was she loved the way she needed to be by parents who went through two world wars?

Of course, when I was young, those thoughts never came to my mind. In those days, I disliked her so much and wanted nothing more than to get away from her. Only much later in life did the questions come. The passage of time brings more understanding and compassion. Today, I wish I could get the answers to so many, many questions that will forever remain unanswered.

Lydia and I continued our lives at Oma and Opa's. When I returned from my stay in the mountains, she was ten years old and I was almost fifteen. I enrolled in a new school. Times had changed, the war was behind us and no one questioned any longer where one came from. I made new friends, loved school, and had plans for the future. My asthma attacks never returned after my stay in Chamonix. And so, the carefree years finally started.

I have not mentioned my friend Jean Bor. Jean's parents were friends of my grandparents throughout my growing-up years. They owned a restaurant and bar on the outskirts of Metz. Everyone had always said that Jean and I would be married someday. He was always there for me as an older brother would have been, and more or less grew up together. He was five years older than me. When I was old enough, we would go dancing together and he would bring me home by midnight, as requested by Oma.

Figure 26.   Jean Borr, 1960.

However, tragedy struck. He was twenty-four years old when he was killed in a car accident on New Year's Eve in 1960. For many years, I could not celebrate a New Year's Eve without thinking of him. So young, a life full of promise. I wonder today what my life would have been had we married. I saw him one last time on his deathbed, all bandaged up, unrecognizable. I kissed his forehead and will never forget the cold, icy feeling of his skin. He was gone; we would never laugh and dance together again. I felt so lost and lonely.

I did not attend his funeral, I could not face it. I did not want to sit there at church listening to the story of his life and hear people cry.

I went alone to the cemetery the next day, and there I sat by his tombstone for what seemed like hours, talked to him and cried my heart out. I knew he understood why I did not attend the funeral.

I walked out of the cemetery and stopped by my little friend Christa's tombstone. I have never returned since.

I loved nursing school and wanted to study pediatrics. However, in my second year of nursing, I had a bout of eczema on my hands and arms. I had to take a break from school, so I found a job on an American military base to have a little income for a few months.

Figure27.   The scene of the accident.

It turned out I never went back to nursing and kept working on the base. I was nineteen, and it was fun working with all those GIs. I held different positions, from KP (Kitchen Police) as it was called, to snack bar attendant, to switchboard operator.

One night a couple of girlfriends and I went out dancing in the nearby city of Strasbourg.

We went to a well-known dance hall and bar. It must have been during the month of March, 1957 or 1958. I don't remember exactly. As we sat at the bar, we saw two American GIs at the other end.

One was very good looking, with dark hair, and the other seemed lost in his thoughts and was drinking heavily. The dark-haired one came over and asked me to dance. He was a good dancer and was humming a song in my ear.

I wish to this day I could remember the song. At that time, I wasn't impressed in the least, thinking it was just another American GI.

Later, after they had left, the barman asked us, "Do you know who these two gentlemen were?" Of course we didn't. He said,

"It was Marlon Brando and Dean Martin." I thought, so what, never heard of them. Not getting a reaction from us, the barman shrugged and continued pouring beers. It was not until years later, when I came to the US, that I found out who they were, and that I had danced with a famous singer and actor. At the time, they had been filming a World War II movie, *The Young Lions*.

Figure28. Dean Martin 1957 (Public domain photo).

39
MY LIFE CHANGES AGAIN

A year after working on the military base, I met a soldier in the American Air Force, John Wilson. We started dating. He was good looking and the girls I worked with were envious. I introduced him to my grandparents, who liked him right away. It became a ritual for him to have dinner with us several times a week. My Oma would cook special meals, and she would often say, "The poor boy is so far from home, we need to spoil him."

We went out together for several months until one evening he proposed to me. Not only was I shocked, but I did not know what to say. In my mind, thoughts were going around: Do I really love him? Love him enough to follow him to his country? If I accept, I could still change my mind.

I said "YES!" without being serious about it.

A few days later, he put an engagement ring on my finger, to the great joy of Oma and Opa. This was February 1962, and he wanted to get married that summer. Again, I thought, why not? I can still change my mind. But in March of that year, I found out I was pregnant.

Oh! God!! Now what??

I went to the doctor, who confirmed my pregnancy. After my appointment, I walked the town for hours, wondering how I was going to announce this at home. What did I get myself into?

I did not want to leave my country. Oh God!! What to do now?

When I got home that evening, I told my Oma. I could not look at her. An unmarried pregnant woman was, in those days, a shame to her family and an outcast. She looked into my eyes and said, "You have two choices, marry him or leave this house." Now there was no way out.

Figure29. John Wilson, 1962.

We planned the wedding for July, a few months later. John needed permission from his colonel, and the paperwork took time. Also, a member of his family had to be my sponsor for coming to America; this turned out to be his father. It seemed as if his entire family was rejoicing and I was the one dreading it. This was turning into a nightmare, as reality hit me more and more. I would have to leave my family and friends, go to another country—what did I get myself into? I thought perhaps I could have a miscarriage, an accident could happen, anything. But nothing went wrong and my pregnancy went on.

We were married on July 7, 1962. I did not show yet and was able to wear a white dress, which my mother paid for. When she found out about my pregnancy, she was happy for me and immediately said she would buy the dress. I don't know how she got the money, but we went shopping together and found the right one. It had to be a knee-length dress. No way would a full-length white dress be acceptable in my condition.

I'd had very little contact with my mother in recent years, but she would show up now and then at my grandparents' and try to get closer. I felt sorry for her at times.

She was in very poor health, skin and bones, but her way of life had not changed; the drinking and smoking had continued.

I made it clear to her that she would be invited to the wedding only if she promised not to drink and embarrass me and the family. And of course, Albert, her husband, would not be invited.

She kept her promise and did not have a drop of alcohol that day.

Early on the morning of the wedding, I went up to our little church and sat outside on a bench in the gardens. Little birds were flying all around me. I wished I could be one of them and fly far away, leaving all this nightmare behind. Again my life was changing, but not in the way I would have wanted or dreamed. It was all my fault. What had I done! How could I have been so foolish and irresponsible?

Figure 30. Annita, 1962.

I sat there for over an hour before I walked back home. With my stomach in a knot and my throat tight, I prepared myself for the wedding.

Family members and friends came; no one guessed how I was feeling inside, not even John, whom I had never seen happier than on that day. I guess for him it was very different than it was for me; I knew he truly was in love with me. He was proud to go back to his country with a French bride and a baby, as he often said. I had communicated as well as I could via letters with his parents and siblings; my English left a lot to be desired, but I tried my best. They were excited to meet me and wrote, "HURRY TO COME HOME." Again, I thought surely I would find a way to avoid going to America. There had to be a way.

I worked at the base switchboard until about six weeks before the baby was due. I was feeling well and had an easy pregnancy. Having always been very slim, I now felt like a whale. My due date was January 5, 1963. Of course, in those days there were no tests to know the sex of the baby. I hoped for a little girl, while John hoped for a boy.

Christmas came. The last one I was to spend with my family and in my country. The paperwork for my visa, passport and other documents was in the making, and I kept hoping that something would prevent me from leaving. Perhaps, because I was the daughter of an SS officer, the American government would not let me into the country. I was dreaming, of course.

New Year's Eve came, and we spent it at Oma and Opa's and went home early. I was feeling very tired and had a severe backache. John went to bed at 10:00 p.m. I stayed up to see the new year come in, my last one at home. I stood in the cold on our balcony and listened to the church bells ring in the year 1963. With tears streaming down my face, I wondered what my future held in store.

Finally, I went to bed, to be awakened at 5:00 a.m. with the first labor pains and my waters breaking. The clinic was next door to our apartment and I wanted to get there right away. But the baby did not come until 10:10 p.m. It was a long day; I had a natural childbirth, which meant absolutely no drugs. It had been my choice, and I had prepared for it for months by attending exercise classes. It was a long labor, lasting seventeen hours. I wanted to be alone and asked John to go home. He would be notified when it was time.

Karen Linda came into the world on New Year's Day. Only a mother can express the feeling of holding in her arms for the first time the child that grew in her womb for nine months.

I loved her immediately. I counted her fingers and toes to make sure they were all there before they took her to the nursery for the night and I was able to sleep.

The next morning was her first feeding. I loved holding my Karina, whose name later changed to Karen once in America. While she was suckling, her little fingers wrapped around my thumb. I could not have loved her more. I knew I would do the right thing for her by going to her father's country. Oma and Opa came later and were ecstatic to be great-grandparents for the first time.

When I went home a few days later, Opa would come by every morning around ten o'clock to visit with me. He would hold the baby and sing to her, which was a new image of my Opa. Or he would send me out of the house to have some time to myself while he babysat.

The months went by too fast. I had to face the fact that my departure was getting closer and closer. All the papers were in order and nothing was holding me back from leaving, as I had hoped. July 28, 1963, was approaching. John had been transferred back to the US, to a place unknown to me—Montgomery, Alabama.

Before we were to go to Alabama, he had thirty days' leave, and we would visit and stay with his family in South Dakota.

American friends I knew from the base were telling me I would not like Alabama; it was hot and muggy and in the middle of the civil rights movement. I had no clue what that meant and no idea what they were talking about. Everyone told me that New York, Chicago or San Francisco would have been preferable for me.

I knew nothing of the United States, but I was to learn quickly once I arrived.

In May, the movers came to pack our things to be sent to the States. We moved in with Oma and Opa for the last six weeks, my last time living at home. I packed the most important things, mostly those that held memories, such as my books, music, and photos. I wondered if I would take Dora, my doll, with me, but decided against it. She was part of a past to be forgotten. The morning we vacated the apartment, I said goodbye to her, sat her on top of the outside trash can, and never looked back as we drove off.

I enjoyed every minute with Oma and Opa, not knowing when or if I would ever return home. America was so far away, and other French girls I knew who had married had not been able to return home as they had wished. The ones who did come to visit did not want to go back and divorced once in France. I did not know what to expect and was scared. Here I was, going so far away with a man I knew very little of. I had no knowledge of his family or lifestyle. I knew that no member of my family would ever visit; it was too far away and too expensive.

I went to see my mother one last time. It was the saddest sight. She lived in a different apartment now, much nicer and cleaner. She was very ill and looked so small in her bed. I felt sorry for her and had to hold back my tears. She had never seen Karina.

Due to her illness, she was too contagious to be near the baby. John had stayed down in the street with Karina in her carriage while I went up to her apartment to see her. I only stayed a few minutes, trying to comfort her by saying that if she got better, perhaps she could come see us in America. She just smiled sadly; we both knew this would never happen. When I left, she asked me to help her out of bed so she could go to the window and see the baby down below. I held her in my arms; she was like a brittle doll, so skinny, so fragile. I did not want to hug her too hard for fear of breaking her. She cried and said only, "Forgive me."

I left, and once on the street, I looked up at the window where she lived. There she was, a ghost of a woman, sticking a long skinny arm out the window in a last goodbye. I waved back at her, knowing I would never see her again. I held back my tears and walked away with my baby and husband.

She died that same year, on December 24, 1963. She had been born on December 26, 1922, the day after Christmas, and died the day before Christmas. She was only forty-one years old.

When I received the news, I could not even cry. I promised myself to never mention the past to anyone. In time I would forget, I thought. Little does one know what a burden the past can be for the rest of a lifetime, how the ghosts stay with us. And contrary to what I thought or promised myself, I was never able to forget.

Figure31. My Grandparents (Oma and Opa) and my daughter Karina, 1963.

40
AMERICA

July 28, 1963, was for me one of the saddest of days. All my family gathered at my grandparents' to bid me goodbye. Some envied me. In their eyes, I was going far away, to a country where many had dreams of going. We hugged, kissed and cried; I could not let go of them.

A military car came to take us to the airport. I remember looking out the back window and seeing my family crying and waving goodbye. I was sobbing; all I could think was that I would never see my family and country again. The only one missing was my Opa. He was behind the living room window on the second floor, waving. I could only imagine his pain. He, who was always there for me, could not face my departure. To this day I still have his letters, but I cannot bring myself to read them again.

A military plane took us from Frankfurt, Germany, to New York. I was holding Karina and clinging to her, looking at the door at the front of the plane, thinking that as long as the door was open I could still run out. When the door closed, it sounded like the lid of a coffin. I watched through my tears as the runway went by and the plane took off. Below, I saw my country disappear little by little. The rooftops, the church steeples, and then nothing but clouds. God! How I cried and cried. Someone said to me, "You will love America, you'll see." I almost hated the person who said that. How could I ever love another country but my own?

It was a long flight, about eighteen hours before we arrived in New York. Karina had slept almost the entire time; she was seven months old. There was a very nice gentleman in the seat in front of us. He had heard me crying and offered to hold the baby for a while. I let him have her and heard him sing to her; I thought it was kind of him.

Figure 32. Jimmy Dean, 1966 (Public domain image).

John told me he was someone well known in the US by the name of Jim Dean. I had no clue of who he was and could not have cared less at the time. It was only many months later, when I saw him on television, that I realized who he was, as well as recognizing Dean Martin and Marlon Brando.

Whoa! Now I was impressed. I had danced with Dean Martin, and I wished I could remember what he sang into my ear that night. Now Karina had been sung to by Jim Dean.

We arrived in New York; it felt so strange and foreign. It looked nothing like home.

Those tall buildings hiding the sky, the street noises and strange language, the differently dressed people. We stayed overnight and flew out the next day to South Dakota. I remember thinking, I am French by birth, German by heritage and soon to be American, but not by choice.

We landed in the little town of Huron, South Dakota, after flying over miles and miles of empty land, with nothing to see. I thought I was flying over the steppes of Russia. Before we landed, I saw a little airport below with what looked like a single hangar and a group of perhaps a dozen people.

As we exited the plane, I realized that all these people were my husband's family and friends. They all ran up to him while I waited in the background with Karina in my arms.

Finally, his mom and dad came over and took the baby from me, and I was introduced to the family. I noticed how the women were looking at me from head to toe. I guess my attire puzzled them. I wore a tight-fitting skirt above the knees, and high heels that were uncomfortably digging into the soft dirt. I noticed they were all wearing jeans and tennis shoes.

The weather felt unbearable. I was not used to the heat and high humidity and was very relieved when the air conditioning in the car cooled me off. Karina was screaming her head off and perspiring, and my mother-in-law was holding her in the front seat, but soon handed her back to me. We left the little town and headed out to the country.

I had never seen such vast land; it went on and on without a single home for miles.

Finally, some farms were visible, cows here and there, and miles of cornfields. I felt as if I had landed on the moon.

All I remember from that first day was the heat, the landscape and arriving at my in-laws' farm exhausted. There were lots of cows, horses and pigs. We entered the farmhouse and were shown to our bedroom. There was a small window air conditioner in the living room but nothing in the bedroom, and the air was stifling. I laid Karina in a little crib, undressed her to her diapers, and wished I could take my clothes off as well. Karina fell asleep, and I sat on the bed and started crying as John came in. He held me and said, "I know it's all new to you, but we will only be here for a couple of weeks. I promise Alabama will be better."

I have forgotten how the days after that went by. All I remember was the terrible heat, sometimes 105 to 115 degrees. I could not sleep at night, and had no appetite. I ate corn for the first time in my life. In France, I thought corn was grown for pigs and had no clue that this was an American staple. I missed wine with my meals. Only milk, Kool-Aid or water was served.

I wanted home so bad, but here I was, stuck in the middle of prairies and cornfields.

As soon as John bought a car, I insisted on learning to drive. It wasn't as easy as I thought because the county roads were gravel and it was easy to slip and slide. But I was determined to learn, and learn I did.

41
MY FIRST DAYS ON THE FARM

John and I had a sort of second wedding celebration. He had a large family, and a hall had been rented to accommodate about two hundred people. Everyone wanted to hear me talk, made me repeat things—they said the way I spoke was so cute. I felt like they were making fun of me.

Figure 33. Arrival at in-laws on the farm in South Dakota, 1963.

MY FIRST DAYS ON THE FARM | 239

At one point, Father Wilson came to me and said he had a surprise wedding gift for us. Told me he and his wife were giving us four pigs as a wedding present. I was speechless, smiled politely and thanked him. Later that night, I asked my husband what his dad was thinking of. Four pigs? How would we fit them into our car? We had luggage, a baby and four pigs to take to Alabama? What were we to do with pigs? I never hear my husband laugh as loud.

Figure34. Indian Chief at Mt. Rushmore, S.D. 1963.

"We are not taking the pigs with us. This week, Dad and I are going to the county fair to sell them. The proceeds from the sale are our wedding gift." That was only the beginning of learning about farm life. Today when I think back on it, I still have to laugh at that conversation and the many mistakes one makes in a foreign country.

Figure35. My first farm work duty upon arrival at in-laws farm.

In mid-August, we left and started the long trip to the South. It took us three days of driving, again in terrible heat and with no air conditioning in the car. We would drive mostly at night and sleep during the day in air-conditioned motels.

What was most shocking to me was driving along the Mississippi River and seeing black men chained at the ankles in cotton fields. There were many white men as well, but they were not chained.

Figure36.   My first donkey ride at in-laws farm.

I asked why the black people were chained and not the white. John explained they were prisoners and that only those who were black had to be chained. This upset me very much and I called it prejudice. I had a lot to learn. This was 1963 in the Deep South, with its entrenched racist policies.

Figure37.   Selma March, Montgomery, Alabama. 1965 (Public domain image).

MY FIRST DAYS ON THE FARM | 241

We arrived in Montgomery and stayed in base housing overnight. The permanent base house we were allotted would not be available for a couple of months. We found a rental apartment outside the base for the next four months until we could move into our new home. The climate was hot and muggy; one had to stay indoors all day in the air conditioning until late in the evening, when a little relief finally came.

There were enormous bugs called cockroaches. I called them animals. No matter how clean the house was kept, they were everywhere. They came out at night from the drains, or they could be found in cupboards. It was a nightmare for me. I once ran over to my next-door neighbor and told him there was an animal that had run under the sofa. He grabbed his gun and I thought, "Oh! My God! That's how they kill them?" The poor man felt so embarrassed when he found out it was a roach.

Of course, homesickness took over. I was sad all the time and started losing weight. Across the street from us was a couple with a child Karina's age, a little boy by the name of Percy.

I became friends with the family, but my husband told me it was not a good idea for me to be seen with them because they were black. It did not go well with me to be told with whom I could or could not associate. I stayed friends with them for the entire four years we lived there. I hated injustice and made it well known to those who tried to convince me otherwise.

In 1965, I participated in the Selma-Montgomery march for a distance of perhaps eight miles.

The march was part of a series of civil rights protests. There were three protest marches held that year, from March 7 through March 25, along the fifty-four miles of highway from Selma to Montgomery.

Nonviolent activists organized the protests to demonstrate the desire of African American citizens to exercise their constitutional right to vote, and to end racist policies.

I joined the march, heading for the state capitol in Montgomery on the last day. Some other white people were marching as well, but very few. I can only say that the activists were very peaceful and marched without causing a disturbance. Bystanders were calling the marchers names, insulting them. It was appalling.

Time moved on slowly, so slowly, and I was miserable. A year after coming to the States, I went back with my baby Karina to France. It was wonderful to be home again, with family and friends, my way of life, my language. I saw my father and Irma, his wife, a few times, against my grandparents' wishes. Karina was then two years old and missed her daddy a lot.

John had bought an open round-trip ticket. At first I thought I would not return to the States, that I would find a job in France and start a new life. But it was not that easy. I felt guilty taking Karina away from her father. Oma was very controlling and I could do nothing without her approval. Five weeks after I arrived, I told Oma I was returning to the States. She begged me to stay at least another week, fearing that she would never see us again due to her age. She was right. I never saw Oma again; she passed away three years later. I guess we were meant to stay a week longer. I am glad we did, because our connecting flight crashed after takeoff from New York.

I remember reading about it when I returned to the States.

I resumed my life in Montgomery and started making a few friends, mostly European women married to Americans. For the next few years, it helped to have people from home, sharing our loneliness and raising our children together.

I also met a middle-aged American couple who took me under their wing. The Watsons were a lovely pair. Mr. Watson was the administrator of Montgomery Baptist Hospital, and I got a job there in nursing thanks to him. It helped a lot to be working and meeting people.

However, Karina had severe bouts of bronchitis. I had to quit work eventually to be home with her full-time. I missed my job but decided to take classes to improve my American English.

Four years later, John was being discharged from the Air Force. He had a choice; he could reenlist and be sent to San Francisco, or he could leave the military. I wanted to go to San Francisco and begged him to reenlist. But he wanted to go back home to South Dakota and work for his brother, who owned a trucking company. I did not want to go back there, but no matter how I approached him, it did no good. Off we went to South Dakota.

While he looked for a house in Sioux Falls, which was three hours away from his parents' farm in Saint Lawrence, I stayed with them. It took him almost six months to find the right home; rentals were hard to come by in the mid-sixties. During that time, he worked in Sioux Falls all week and came back on weekends to the farm.

What can I say about my six months on the farm... It was again a big change for me. I was sure I would die of loneliness and boredom. Karina, at age four, was in seventh heaven with her grandparents, who spoiled her. Once a week I was granted the big treat of visiting the little town of Miller, where my mother-in-law would do laundry, shop and meet with other farm women while the men went to local bars to shoot pool and drink beer.

I have to admit I learned a lot from my mother-in-law. She taught me to sew and cook the American way. I sewed for Karina and myself, finding vogue patterns from France. My sisters-in-law asked me to make dresses for them. Those activities made time go by so much faster.

But there was nowhere to go and wear my new dresses, other than on the farm or to the little town on Saturdays, where I was known as the French girl. I was probably the most fashionable woman for miles around. Ha!

The six months finally came to an end, and we moved into a house in the small city of Sioux Falls. I had a life of my own again and immediately went in search of a job. I was hired at Sioux Valley Hospital, where I worked in Labor and Delivery as a nurse practitioner. I loved my job and made new friends. One of them was Karen Rohr, my supervisor. She was to be my best friend for many years to come. Life was not so bad, but I was still very homesick and saved money to go home whenever I could.

Karina's name quickly changed to Karen; no one could pronounce her French name right.

In September 1967, I became pregnant. This time, I was ready for another baby and was elated at the news.

The following February, in 1968, Oma passed away. I immediately flew home. Opa was not healthy and was so lost without Oma. I could only stay a few weeks, and I spent most of my time with Opa, trying to comfort him and listening to past memories. What a lonely man he had become, and so fragile. I hated to think of leaving him. I was worried for his future with his daughter Georgette, who had him move in with her. He told me he wanted to get back to his own home, but Georgette and my aunt Cécile had already emptied the apartment and sold most of the furniture. He had no place to go at that point and was ill. It broke my heart the day I held him tight for the last time and saw tears in his eyes. But I had to go back to the States; I was almost seven months pregnant at that time. He understood, but our last moments together were so sad. I wondered if I would see him again, this man who had raised me and who once was so strong.

Shortly after I left, I found out his daughters had put him in a nursing home, the poorest and cheapest one in Metz. Opa would write me and tell me how lonely and sick he was, begging me to come home and get him out of that sordid place. I could not do anything, being so very far away. I wrote him several times a week and waited impatiently for his letters, which made me cry bitterly each time. He lasted less than a year before he passed away. It was almost a relief for me to know he was no longer suffering. How I missed this wonderful man who had always been there for me and who was the only father figure I ever had. When he needed me the most, I was so far away, and could do nothing to help him make his last days comfortable and peaceful. To this day, I miss him and will always carry his love in my heart.

Nathalie was born June 18, 1968, in Sioux Falls, South Dakota. With her little fat face and dark brown hair, it was an immediate bonding between her and me. To this day, she is not only my daughter, but also my very best friend.

We stayed in South Dakota for three more years. During that time, I became an American citizen. It took a couple of years of studying the history of the United States before I could apply, and then I was contacted to appear before a judge. There were one hundred questions on the list, and of those, only ten would be asked at random. That seemed very few, but one had to be able to answer any of the possible questions. I was ready and passed my test with flying colors.

It was not my happiest day; I felt I had turned my back on my country by becoming a citizen of another one. I did it mainly for my children. A lawyer had told me that if anything went wrong, such as a divorce, my husband and his family could claim custody of my girls and I could not take them out of the country, being a foreign citizen.

This was the law in those days. There was no way I would ever be separated from my children, and the best way to avoid that was for me to become a citizen. The best part was that I did not lose my French citizenship; I have dual nationalities.

In those days, the number of people seeking citizenship was smaller than today. There might have been thirty or so applicants in the state of South Dakota at that time. Today that number is in the hundreds, and they pay up to three thousand dollars, I heard. It cost me about fifty dollars in 1968.

That same year, John was transferred to Des Moines, Iowa, to work at another company his brother owned. It was hard again to leave my new friends and job and start all over in another state. It seemed as if I would never have stability in my life. But I immediately made new friends a few months after I arrived.

The winters were harsh and very snowy. Blizzards were the norm, and sometimes one could not get out of the house for several days at a time. The summers were hot and humid. Two of my sisters-in-law lived outside Des Moines, which gave John some family to be around. My Dad and Irma (whom I called Mama) visited from France for the first time. It was wonderful to have my family with me if even for a short time.

We lived in Des Moines for four years before John was transferred again, this time to Denver, Colorado. I immediately loved that state because of the proximity to the mountains. I told him it was the end of the road for me, I would never move again. Finally I had mountains, beauty around me and a great climate to live in. I quickly made new friends again, mostly French and German women, which gave me a sense of belonging. We joined German clubs, and it became an international group, which I loved and would for many years to come.

I learned how to cross-country ski and snowshoe in the winter months and hike the mountains in the summer. I also took up photography. I finally felt at home and was always on the go. Lots of weekends, I went dancing at the German clubs with friends. I took secretarial science courses at the community college and found work. It was not difficult, especially since I spoke three languages. I did every job from file clerk, to records manager, to private secretary of the president of a company called Western Nuclear, a subsidiary of Phelps Dodge in the late seventies.

Although I was keeping myself busy, my homesickness never left me, and I traveled to France every year. I needed to be with my family, and returning to my culture was so important for me.

As the years went by, my relationship with my husband deteriorated. He was a good man, a good provider, but he left the discipline of the girls to me entirely, as well as the finances.

We had so little in common; he did not care for mountain activities or traveling. I did a lot with the girls or by myself. When Karina left and married, Nathalie and I did a lot together until she, too, left and got married. That's when my husband and I separated at my demand, but we stayed married for eight years after the separation. We were almost like good friends during that time; he insisted I keep the house and he took care of the household expenses. It was very decent of him. He had met another woman, and he married her a few years after our divorce in 1992.

42
ROBERT

The first year after the divorce was the most difficult. I was alone for the first time, but as time went on, I began enjoying my life.

Eight years later, my daughter Nathalie introduced me to a wonderful gentleman, Robert Rodgers. I never wanted to remarry, and if I did it would have been a European man, I thought. But life decided differently.

Robert and I got along very well from the moment we met, and we married less than two years later.

We loved traveling the world together. In 2004, we visited my family in Europe, who loved Robert right away. The only thing I missed was dancing, which he was not fond of. We retired the same year, and took our first retiree trip to Ireland. From then on, we took many international trips and cruises. We enjoyed Mexico most of all, where we still return sometimes twice a year.

Robert also has two daughters. Margaret, the oldest, now has two boys, Peyton and Jacob. Mallissa, the youngest, has twins, Maggie and Mathew, and another boy, Sam.

In the year 2000, we built our first home in Grand Lake, Colorado, a custom-made Swiss chalet. We shared it part time with a townhouse we also had built in Arvada. For almost twenty years, we enjoyed going back and forth between the two homes, had many friends in both areas, and enjoyed visits from family and friends from Europe. It was my dream home. We made many friends in the tiny mountain town of Grand Lake, had great times, and enjoyed many outdoor activities. However, little by little, over the years, some friends left for warmer climates and some, alas, passed away.

Meanwhile, my sister Elvira came back into my life. My brother passed away at age fifty-two of cancer, and we met at his funeral. We bonded very quickly and to this day, are very close.

In 2017, Robert and I moved up to the mountains full time. But it did not work as planned, mainly on my part. The winters were endless, as was the solitude. We moved back to Denver. It was a blessing in disguise, as we were to find out later.

I will always miss the home we built with so much love, the beauty of the mountains, my pet foxes, the wildlife all around. We moved back to Denver in the spring of 2019, and in 2020 we sold the mountain home.

Six weeks after we sold the home, a devastating fire engulfed the valley and the surrounding mountains. Our beautiful chalet burned down along with 366 homes in the area.

Several months went by before I could go back and see the devastation. It was awful, nothing but ashes left. My heart broke, as did Robert's. Everything gone—the beautiful chalet, the wood cabin he had built himself, with so much love, on the next acre—only ashes left.

I could not believe that twenty years of memories lay in ashes. Where were my foxes, the deer, the bears that had roamed the surrounding woods?

Our children Karen and Nathalie, their husbands, and our grandchildren, Sydney, Mariah, Derik and Cailey, were all part of those beautiful years.

The devastation made me think of my childhood—fire, destruction, death—all over again.

Although I have been blessed with many years of good health, there have been some challenges. In 2012, I was diagnosed with chronic myeloid leukemia and was on chemotherapy for five years. I lost my hair and a lot of body strength until I decided on my own to stop the drug, against my oncologist's recommendations. Six years later, I am still clear of this terrible disease.

However, there was another curve in the road in 2023. I was diagnosed with breast cancer in my right breast, stage 2. I had a lateral mastectomy, followed by six weeks of daily radiation that did a tough job on my body and psychological outlook. I was grateful to have Robert as my strong support and at my side daily, as well as my daughter Nathalie, other family members and so many, many friends without whom I don't know how I would have pulled through.

Life has blessed me with four grandchildren on my side:
Sydney and Mariah, Karen's children.
Derik and Cailey, Nathalie's children.

Seven great-grandchildren:
Adleigh and Eleanor, Mariah's children.
Lucy, and Stetson, Sydney's children.
Asher, Hunter and Sawyer, Derik's children.

On Robert's side, there are five grandchildren:
Mathew and Margaret (twins), and Sam, by his daughter Mallissa.
Peyton and Jacob, by his daughter Margaret.
A total of nine grandchildren and seven great-grandchildren.

I guess my life has not been in vain. I have a lot to be grateful for.

How does one end a memoir? Time goes by; how many years are left? It is, and has been, an interesting life; there are no regrets. Life shaped me into what I am today. The horizon that once was so far ahead is now within arm's reach. I still miss my homeland and my family there. Sadly, so far away.

I think of the following words from the hymn *The fire has never gone out* by Morris Stancil:

THE FLAME HAS FLICKERED, BUT THE FIRE HAS NEVER GONE OUT.

These words have helped me to never give up. I am grateful for everything that is and was my life.

Figure 38. Annita and Robert.

Photos
CHALET

MY CHALET

YOU LEFT ME STANDING ALONE AND CRYING IN THE WIND.

BUT, YOU ARE STILL HERE, YOU HAVE NOT LEFT MY HEART.

FOREVER YOU WILL BE WITH ME IN THIS BEAUTIFUL VALLEY.

I AM WALKING THE LONELY DESERTED AND DESTROYED FOREST,

SEARCHING FOR WHAT ONCE WAS AND NEVER WILL BE AGAIN.

WHERE YOU ONCE STOOD IS NOW ONLY EMPTINESS AND ASHES.

ONLY THE STARS AT NIGHT REMAIN THE SAME.

Our Chalet, Chamonix.

Coyote Lodge that Robert built by hand.

Our mountain wildlife.

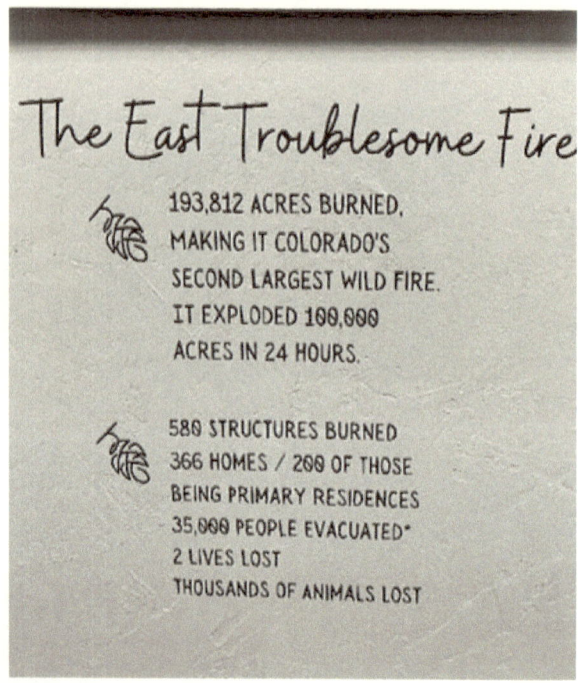

Winds over two hundred miles per hour, temperatures over two thousand degrees.

Figure39. U.S. Department of AgricultureU.S. Forest Service/USDA. (Public domain photo)

What was left of the Chalet.

ABOUT THE AUTHOR

As a daughter of a Nazi SS, Annita Bosse Rodgers grew-up in Eastern France, the Province of Lorraine. It was at the height of World War II and her province was then under German rules. As the daughter of a French woman and an SS soldier, she suffered throughout her early years of rejection, abuse and shame. At age 22, she married an American Soldier and followed him to the U.S. with her seven month old baby girl. Another baby girl was born six years later. Annita became an American citizen in 1967.

Today, remarried for a second time, she lives with her husband in Denver, Colorado. The publishing of her father's memoirs and her own, is the history of suffering of divided families and countries.

JOURNEY INSTITUTE PRESS

Journey Institute Press is a non-profit publishing house created by authors to flip the publishing model for new authors. Created with intention and purpose to provide the highest quality publishing resources available to authors whose stories might otherwise not be told.

JI Press focusses on women, BIPOC, and LGBTQ+ authors without regard to the genre of their work.

As a Publishing House, our goal is to create a supportive, nurturing, and encouraging environment that puts the author above the publisher in the publishing model.

Storytellers Publishing is an Imprint of Journey Institute Press, a division of 50 in 52 Journey, Inc.

NOTE: The world of publishing has changed dramatically. This has also affected authors and their ability to let readers know about their books. Today, most people buy books based on word of mouth.

If you would like to help this author, please consider leaving an honest review of this book on retail sites and book community sites.

www.ingramcontent.com/pod-product-compliance
Lightning Source LLC
Chambersburg PA
CBHW030241010526
44107CB00030B/1294/J